Scholar-Activism and Land Struggles

Praise for this book

An exceptionally important book, which will have an important and influential audience amongst scholar-activists engaged with land and agrarian issues worldwide.

Ian Scoones, Institute of Development Studies, University of Sussex

You'll hear the term 'instant classic' used to refer to Borras and Franco's profound meditation on the role of academics working with movements for agrarian change. It's true that this short book will immediately and deservedly become part of the critical agrarian studies canon, but it's also a work that's far from instant. It draws on decades of combined scholarship and activism, at the highest levels and with the highest stakes. The result is a distillation of two lifetimes' work, in a few powerful, memorable pages. I wish I'd had it at the start of my career, but it'll never be too late to reflect on the ideas in *Scholar-Activism and Land Struggles*.

Raj Patel, University of Texas at Austin

With an expansive historical and intellectual framing, and animated with proximate examples, Jun and Jenny capture the real difficulties and tensions, but also the potency, of scholar-activism – and how it can, and does, strengthen agrarian struggles. I cannot think of people better placed to guide, and challenge, us to build this praxis.

Ruth Hall, PLAAS, University of the Western Cape, Cape Town

This book has been much needed for decades and it is a relief to have it now. It is the most serious discussion of scholar-activism that I know of, addressing its aspirations, limitations and contradictions. It does so in a solid and convincing way that reflects the life-long engagement and experiences of the authors who have ample experience in critically connecting knowledge institutions, international networks and radical agrarian movements.

Jan Douwe van der Ploeg, author, The New Peasantries

Using lucid language, this book takes us through contentious history and present of agrarian political struggles, offering a principled and yet inclusive understanding. Students and activists working for social justice and for a non-capitalist future would find this book to be both an inspiring mentor and an impassioned friend.

Yan Hairong, Tsinghua University, Beijing

This book presents a rich history of sustained engagement with (agrarian) social movements by two "critically engaged" scholar-activists. It is a *tour de force* at the intersection of scholar-activism and land struggles. Students, academics, and activists interested in the dynamics of agrarian politics in the Global South should read this book.

Walter Chambati, Sam Moyo African Institute for Agrarian Studies

This book is about the ways in which engaged scholarship and practical politics shape each other, and about the contradictions, tensions, and conflicts therein involved. But it is much more: a powerful reflection on the politics of land and the role that both theory and practice have in achieving a more just world. It is a gift for anyone interested in agrarian justice.

Diana Ojeda, La Universidad de los Andes, Bogota

Borras and Franco blend their extensive field and institutional experiences in a deliberative ethical guide for scholar-activists engaging with agrarian and urban land movements, and a corporate academy. This watershed monograph offers two fundamental directives: recognizing historically contextual experiences of specific agrarian communities as critical to the knowledge politics of movement struggles; and, reappraising the methodological implications of ongoing capitalist transformations of agrarian worlds, with diversified property relations threatening human and producer-labor rights in an ecologically challenged era. The authors provide a powerful and timely intervention regarding the global recasting of landscapes of contention and the domain of agrarian studies.

Philip McMichael, Cornell University and author of Food Regimes and Agrarian Questions

Jenny and Jun have an amazing ability to talk as academics and activists and challenge both in a comradely way. They manage to push us to think beyond concepts, imagination and beliefs towards the radical ideas that are needed and urgent to transform this society into a more just and sustainable one.
Lyda Fernanda, Integracion de Educacion Ambiental y Social (IDEAS), Colombia

A deeply inspiring book that sets the ground for a movement of scholar-activists. While profoundly rooted in agrarian issues, this book is also of tremendous value for environmental justice scholars, degrowth proponents and many more striving not only to better understand but also to transform the contemporary social and environmental challenges of our world.
Arnim Scheidel, Institut de Ciència i Tecnologia Ambientals (ICTA-UAB), Universitat Autònoma de Barcelona

The authors unpack the role of the scholar-activist, the critical contributions they can make to movements, and the tensions, risks, challenges and pitfalls of their work ... The book is a guide for all of those who believe that the point of knowledge is to change the world for the better, and who strive to live their lives according to that commitment.
Pietje Vervest, Hamza Hamouchene, Katie Sandwell Transnational Institute (from the Foreword)

Agrarian Change and Peasant Studies Series

Class Dynamics of Agrarian Change
  by Henry Bernstein, 2010

Peasants and the Art of Farming: A Chayanovian Manifesto
  by Jan Douwe van der Ploeg, 2013

Food Regimes and Agrarian Questions
  by Philip McMichael, 2013

Sustainable Livelihoods and Rural Development
  by Ian Scoones, 2015

Political Dynamics of Transnational Agrarian Movements
  by Marc Edelman and Saturnino M. Borras Jr. 2016

Agrarian Change, Migration and Development
  by Henry Veltmeyer and Raúl Delgado-Wise, 2016

Agroecology: Science and Politics
  by Peter M. Rosset and Miguel A. Altieri, 2017

Speculative Harvests: Financialization, Food and Agriculture
  by Jennifer Clapp and Ryan Isakson, 2018

Counterrevolution: The Global Rise of the Far Right
  by Walden Bello, 2019

Agriculture and the Generation Problem
  by Ben White, 2020

Agrarian Change and Peasant Studies: Little books on big issues

Series editors

Saturnino M. Borras Jr., International Institute of Social Studies (ISS), The Hague, The Netherlands
Sergio Coronado, Center for Research and Popular Education (CINEP), Colombia
Ruth Hall, Institute for Poverty, Land and Agrarian Studies (PLAAS), University of the Western Cape, South Africa
Max Spoor, ISS, The Hague, The Netherlands
Henry Veltmeyer, Universidad Autónoma de Zacatecas, Mexico
Jingzhong Ye, College of Humanities and Development Studies (COHD), China Agricultural University, China

International Editorial Advisory Committee

Duygu Avci, Sabanci University, Turkey
Gonzalo Colque, Fundación Tierra, Bolivia
Alessandra Corrado, University of Calabria, Italy
Raúl Delgado-Wise, Universidad Autónoma de Zacatecas, Mexico
Bernardo Mançano Fernandes, Universidade Estadual Paulista, Presidente Prudente (UNESP), Brazil
Sayaka Funada-Classen, Japan
Hamza Hamouchene, SIYADA Network and Transnational Institute (TNI) MENA Programmes
Shuji Hisano, Kyoto University, Japan
Umut Kocagöz, International Institute of Social Studies (ISS), The Netherlands
Koichi Ikegami, Kindai Universit, Japan
Alexander Nikulin, Russian Presidential Academy of National Economy and Public Administration (RANEPA), Russia
Fatih Özden, Ege University, Turkey

Laksmi Savitri, Samadhya Institute, Indonesia

Sergio Schneider, Universidade Federal do Rio Grande do Sul (UFRGS), Brazil

Wonkyu Song, Research Institute of Agriculture and Peasant Policy, South Korea

Chayan Vaddhanaphuti, Regional Center for Social Science and Sustainable Development (RCSD), University of Chiang Mai, Thailand

Sponsor of the open access ICAS Small Ebook Series Book No. 11

RRUSHES-5 Funded by European Research Council Advanced Grant (Grant No. 834006) and the Transnational Institute (TNI)

Sponsors of the ICAS Small Book Series

Initiatives in Critical Agrarian Studies (ICAS), College of Humanities and Development Studies (COHD) of China Agricultural University, International Institute of Social Studies (ISS) of Erasmus University and PLAAS of the University of the Western Cape

Scholar-Activism and Land Struggles

Saturnino M. Borras Jr. and Jennifer C. Franco

Practical Action Publishing Ltd
25 Albert Street, Rugby,
Warwickshire, CV21 2SD, UK
www.practicalactionpublishing.com

© Saturnino M. Borras Jr. and Jennifer C. Franco, 2023
The moral right of the authors to be identified as the authors of the work have been asserted under sections 77 and 78 of the Copyright Design and Patents Act 1988.

This open access publication is created under a Creative Commons Attribution Non-commercial No-derivatives CC BY-NC-ND licence.
This allows the reader to copy and redistribute the material, but appropriate credit must be given, the material must not be used for commercial purposes, and if the material is transformed or built upon the modified material may not be distributed. For further information see https://creativecommons.org/licenses/by-nc-nd/4.0/legalcode.

Product or corporate names may be trademarks or registered trademarks, and are used only for identification and explanation without intent to infringe.

A catalogue record for this book is available from the British Library.

A catalogue record for this book has been requested from the Library of Congress.

ISBN 978–1-78853–257–0 Paperback
ISBN 978–1-78853–258–7 Hardback
ISBN 978–1-78853–259–4 Electronic book

Citation: Borras, S.M. Jr. and Franco, J.C. (2023) *Scholar-Activism and Land Struggles*, Rugby, UK: Practical Action Publishing <http://doi.org/10.3362/9781788532594>.

Since 1974, Practical Action Publishing has published and disseminated books and information in support of international development work throughout the world. Practical Action Publishing is a trading name of Practical Action Publishing Ltd (Company Reg. No. 1159018), the wholly owned publishing company of Practical Action. Practical Action Publishing trades only in support of its parent charity objectives and any profits are covenanted back to Practical Action (Charity Reg. No. 247257, Group VAT Registration No. 880 9924 76).

The views and opinions in this publication are those of the author and do not represent those of Practical Action Publishing Ltd or its parent charity Practical Action.

Reasonable efforts have been made to publish reliable data and information, but the authors and publisher cannot assume responsibility for the validity of all materials or for the consequences of their use.

Cover image is from the painting "Agrarian Marxism" by the Filipino activist artist Boy Dominguez, 24" × 36", watercolour on paper (2017).

Typeset by vPrompt eServices, India

We dedicate this book to the memory of
Manuel P. Quiambao
(1954–2012)
aka Ka Taning, Gerry Acuña, Steve, Steve Guerrero,
Esteban, Teban, Tebs, Maning
mentor, comrade, friend and *ninong*

Contents

About the authors	xv
Foreword to the series	xvii
Foreword	xxi
Preface	xxv
List of abbreviations	xxix

Chapter 1 Scholars, activists, and agrarian struggles — 1
- Struggles and scholarship — 1
- Historical roots of competing views on agrarian politics and allies — 12
- Historical roots of contemporary agrarian politics — 17
- The current conjuncture — 28

Chapter 2 The politics of land — 35
- Introduction — 35
- The contemporary global land rush — 35
- Broadening the scope of land politics — 38
- Land movements — 43

Chapter 3 Scholar-activism — 55
- Studies about scholar-activism — 56
- Scholar-activism in critical agrarian studies — 69
- Scholar-activism and the academy — 74
- Scholar-activism and political activism — 86

Chapter 4 What is to be done? Future challenges for agrarian scholar-activism — 97
- Aims: Access, equity, autonomy — 102
- Transformative knowledge — 108
- Affirmative action — 115
- Solidarity and internationalism — 117

References — 123

About the authors

Dr Saturnino M. Borras Jr. is professor of agrarian studies at the International Institute of Social Studies (ISS) in The Hague, Distinguished Professor at the College of Humanities and Development Studies at China Agricultural University in Beijing, and an associate at the Transnational Institute (TNI). He is co-author (with Marc Edelman) of *Political Dynamics of Transnational Agrarian Movements* (2016).

Dr Jennifer C. Franco is a researcher at TNI, particularly in the Myanmar-in-Focus programme and the Agrarian and Environmental Justice programme. She is an adjunct professor at the College of Humanities and Development Studies at China Agricultural University in Beijing. She is co-editor with Saturnino M. Borras Jr. of *The Oxford Handbook of Land Politics* (2023).

Foreword to the series

Scholar-Activism and Land Struggles is the eleventh volume in the Agrarian Change and Peasant Studies Series from ICAS (Initiatives in Critical Agrarian Studies).

Together, these eleven books reaffirm the strategic importance and relevance of applying agrarian political economy analytical lenses in critical agrarian studies today. They suggest that succeeding volumes in the series will be just as politically relevant and scientifically rigorous.

A brief explanation of the series will help put the current volume by Borras and Franco into perspective in relation to the ICAS intellectual and political project.

Today, global poverty remains a significantly rural phenomenon, with rural populations comprising three-quarters of the world's poor. Thus the problem of global poverty and the multidimensional (economic, political, social, cultural, gender, environmental, and so on) challenge of ending it are closely linked to rural working people's resistance to the system that continues to generate and reproduce the conditions of rural poverty, and their struggles for sustainable livelihoods. A focus on rural development thus remains critical to development thinking. However, this focus does not mean de-linking rural from urban issues. The challenge is to better understand the linkages between them, partly because the pathways out of rural poverty paved by neoliberal policies and the war on global poverty engaged in and led by mainstream international financial and development institutions, to a large extent, simply replace rural with urban forms of poverty.

Mainstream approaches in agrarian studies are generously financed and thus have been able to dominate the production and publication of research and studies on agrarian issues. Many of the institutions that promote this thinking (such as the World Bank) have also been able to acquire skills in producing and propagating highly accessible and policy-oriented publications that are widely disseminated worldwide. Critical thinkers in leading academic institutions are able to challenge this mainstream approach, but their work is generally confined to academic circles with limited popular reach and impact.

There remains a significant gap in meeting the needs of academics (teachers, researchers, and students), social movement activists, and development practitioners in the Global South and North for scientifically rigorous yet accessible, politically relevant, policy-oriented, affordable books in critical agrarian studies. In response to this need, ICAS has launched this small book series. The idea is to publish 'state-of-the-art' small books that will explain a specific development issue based on key questions, including: What are the current issues and debates in this particular topic? Who are the key scholars/thinkers and actual policy practitioners? How have such positions developed over time? What are the possible future trajectories? What are the key reference materials? Why and how is it important for NGO professionals, social movement activists, official development aid circles, non-governmental donor agencies, students, academics, researchers, and policy experts to critically engage with the key points explained in the book? Each book combines theoretical and practical politics-oriented discussion with empirical examples from different national and local settings.

We aspire and work to make many, if not all, books in the series available in multiple languages in addition to English: Chinese, Spanish, Portuguese, Indonesian, Thai, Japanese, Korean, Italian, Russian, Turkish, and Arabic. The Chinese edition is produced in partnership with the College of Humanities and Development of the China Agricultural University in Beijing, coordinated by Ye Jingzhong; the Spanish edition with the PhD Programme in Development Studies at the Universidad Autónoma de Zacatecas in Mexico, coordinated by Raúl Delgado-Wise and Fundación Tierra in Bolivia coordinated by Gonzalo Colque; the Portuguese edition with the Universidade Estadual Paulista, Presidente Prudente (UNESP) in Brazil, coordinated by

Bernardo Mançano Fernandes, and the Universidade Federal do Rio Grande do Sul (UFRGS) in Brazil, coordinated by Sergio Schneider; the Indonesian edition with Laksmi Savitri; the Thai edition with RCSD of University of Chiang Mai, coordinated by Chayan Vaddhanaputi; the Italian edition coordinated by Alessandra Corrado at the University of Calabria; the Japanese edition coordinated by Shuji Hisano of Kyoto University, Koichi Ikegami of Kindai Universit, and Sayaka-Funada-Classen; the Korean edition with the Research Institute of Agriculture and Peasant Policy and coordinated by Wonkyu Song; the Russian edition with the Russian Presidential Academy of National Economy and Public Administration (RANEPA), coordinated by Alexander Nikulin; the Turkish edition coordinated by Umut Kocagöz and Duygu Avci; and the Arabic edition coordinated by Hamza Hamouchene of TNI.

Given the objectives of the Agrarian Change and Peasant Studies Series, one can easily understand why we are delighted to have this work by Borras and Franco as book 11. The first eleven volumes fit together well in terms of themes, accessibility, relevance and rigour. We are excited about the bright future of this important series!

Book 11 is being released in partnership and collaboration with TNI.

Saturnino M. Borras Jr., Sergio Coronado, Ruth Hall,
Max Spoor, Henry Veltmeyer, and Ye Jingzhong
Series editors

Foreword

We are living through a critical moment for global justice struggles. The effects of the deepening climate crisis are becoming visible to all. Inequality is rampant and growing. State repression and surveillance are increasing. Many proposed 'solutions' to the climate crisis – from carbon markets to agrofuels – will intensify these dynamics as they rely on land-grabbing, extractivism, and the creation of new sacrifice zones and sacrificial peoples around the world, so deepening inequality and multiplying the wealth of the very few. Social movements are struggling not only to block the worst of these advances, but also to build a more just world, to negotiate new relationships with 'nature' and each other, and to resist and roll back the rapacity and destruction of capitalist accumulation. But the challenges that they face are formidable. The need for analyses which are deep, bold, and embedded in peoples' lived realities is increasingly acute as movements struggle to confront new and rapidly-changing realities.

At the same time, the relationship between knowledge, truth, and justice is today deeply fraught. Much-needed struggles about knowledge creation have called into question the roles, structures, and interests of academic institutions; the role of knowledge creation in legitimating and maintaining social and economic power has been exposed and condemned; decolonial, feminist, and indigenous critiques have confronted claims of abstraction and certainty; and the collection and use of data and information are increasingly critical terrains of struggle. In this context there is an urgent need to reveal and recover the emancipatory potential of knowledge, and the transformative power of research and thinking grounded in diverse social realities and explicit commitments to justice.

This book provides a vital and timely contribution to these struggles. With wisdom and humility born of decades of work with and for agrarian and environmental justice movements, the authors unpack the role of the scholar-activist; the critical contributions they can make to movements; and the tensions, risks, challenges, and pitfalls of their work. The book does this with special reference to land struggles, recognizing the great and growing importance of these struggles in the context of climate change, and the possibilities they offer for uniting diverse kinds of working people. The book offers a rich theoretical exploration of the role and importance of scholar-activists in relation to agrarian and climate justice struggles in particular. More than this, though, it is a guide for all of those who believe that the point of knowledge is to change the world for the better, and who strive to live their lives according to that commitment.

Collectively, we (the authors of this foreword) have decades of experience navigating the awkward but fertile borderlands between activism and knowledge creation, and bringing scholar-activists together with social movements to build shared arguments, proposals, and knowledge for a better world. We work with young and aspiring scholar-activists and with movements engaged in different grassroots struggles around the world. It is on this basis that we can say with confidence that this book will be an invaluable guide to scholar-activists, whether they are based in academe, embedded in movements, or based in independent activist research institutions like TNI (to which we belong).

We have had the privilege to work alongside Jenny and Jun and watch some of the ideas and questions in this book take shape. Jun is a long-time Fellow of TNI. Jenny has been a part of the Agrarian and Environmental Justice team and of the Myanmar team at TNI for over 10 years and has played a key role in shaping the work of both teams. They each bring over 35 years of knowledge and experience from the many struggles for social justice they have witnessed and taken part in. Through their scholar-activism, they have helped TNI to navigate complex relationships with agrarian and food sovereignty movements around the world, and to build relationships with progressive academics through initiatives like the Emancipatory Rural Politics Initiative, the Land Deal Politics Initiative, and the ICAS, which have embedded TNI in broader scholar-activist networks.

We are deeply grateful to Jun and Jenny for writing this book. It offers a compassionate but uncompromising account of the tensions, challenges, and questions that scholar-activists must confront, which will surely make it required reading for future generations of scholar-activists. At the same time, it offers the promise that the work of confronting these questions is not solitary but collective, and invites us all to put our shoulder to the plough to carry on the work of building a better world.

Pietje Vervest, Hamza Hamouchene, Katie Sandwell
Transnational Institute
January 2023

Preface

This small book is part of our ongoing collaboration in the context of political struggles for agrarian justice over more than 30 years. We started our collaboration in 1992 in the Philippines. Jenny was then a Fulbright scholar conducting her doctoral fieldwork, and Jun was a full-time activist with the *Kilusang Magbubukid ng Pilipinas* (Philippine Peasant Movement), KMP. Since then, we have expanded our work to several other countries, notably, for Jenny, Myanmar. Over time, and on various occasions, we have both worked in three institutional sites of knowledge politics: academic institutions, non-academic independent research institutions, and agrarian movements. Today, Jenny is based at the independent activist research institution TNI, while Jun is based at ISS, both in the Netherlands. However, our individual activist works date back further: in the 1980s–1990s, Jenny worked in Durham, North Carolina and Boston, Massachusetts with student and women's movements, and did solidarity work with non-US left-wing movements; and Jun has been working with radical Philippine peasant movements since the early 1980s, and later, internationally, as part of the process of establishing La Via Campesina in 1993. Our individual and joint works have largely been focused on the politics of land and the role of radical agrarian movements.

Since our collaboration began, we have taken rural working peoples' struggles for social justice as our intellectual and political compass, and scholar-activism as our method of work. It has never been straightforward to be, or to aspire to be, scholar-activists. On countless occasions, both of us have been doubted and dismissed, looked down on and questioned by comrades and colleagues – for being 'too academic' when we worked in primarily activist settings, or 'too activist' in academic settings. But we have tried to see these occasions as steeling moments for us because we always learned new things, albeit often the hard way, on how to become better in what we do and move closer to our scholar-activist ideal. We feel we are not much closer to that ideal, but we also feel that we have journeyed far enough and have gained sufficient critical insights to dare to write a preliminary synthesis of our reflections about scholar-activism and land struggles in the form of this small book.

We see our work as part of a bigger terrain and longer processes of collective intellectual and political activist work. It is not always easy for us to put our names as authors to particular papers when we know that the ideas in those papers are outcomes of social processes in the broad, often amorphous, communities to which we consciously constructed our sense of belonging over time. In this sense, the ideas in this book are not solely our ideas, but were picked up and processed during and from long hours of community conversations, agrarian movement strategy sessions, and informal chats with key movement cadres in the trenches, as well as exchanges with fellow researchers in academia. We cannot comprehensively attribute all the ideas we are putting forward here: even if it were possible to do so, the long list of all the individuals who have participated in such collective intellectual and political work would fill many pages. So, we will not attempt to create a list because we would surely massively fail to do justice to such a community. But we hope that many of our comrades and friends will be able to read this small book, and know that they were part of the process of generating so many of the ideas here. For that we are deeply indebted and grateful.

During the past three decades, many institutions and organizations provided financial support to our scholar-activist work, especially research work. It is impossible to thank them all. But we want to recognize two institutions that played key roles in the process of coming up with the idea for this book and of making it a reality: Jenny's work has received financial support from TNI, and Jun's work from the European Research Council Advanced Grant (Grant No. 834006). We also thank TNI for co-funding this book.

Several parts of this small book draw on previous individual and joint publications. Therefore, we would like to acknowledge ISS, TNI, and the publishers of *Globalizations, Journal of Agrarian Change, Land Use Policy* and *Third World Quarterly*.

Finally, for their critical and very useful comments and suggestions on earlier drafts, we would like to thank Sergio Coronado, Jonathan Fox, Ruth Hall, Phil McMichael, Jesse Ribot, Ian Scoones, and Annie Shattuck. We would like to thank Paula Bownas for the excellent copyediting of the text; and Eva Broer, Veronika Goussatchenko, and Chaya Raghoenath of the ISS Projects Office for all their support to Jun's work. And last but not least, we thank Jutta Mackwell, Rosanna Denning, and Chloe Callan-Foster of Practical Action Publishing for helping this manuscript see the light of day.

Jun & Jenny
The Hague, December 2022

List of abbreviations

BIPOC	Black, Indigenous, People of Colour
BRICS	Brazil, Russia, India, China and South Africa
CASAS	Collective of Agrarian Scholar-Activists in the South
COP	Conference of the Parties
FPIC	Free, Prior and Informed Consent
GMO	Genetically Modified Organism
IAASTD	International Assessment of Agricultural Knowledge, Science and Technology for Development
ICAS	Initiatives in Critical Agrarian Studies
ISS	International Institute of Social Studies
MST	Movement of Landless Workers (Brazil)
NGO	Non-governmental organization
ODA	Official development aid
PLAAS	Institute for Poverty, Land and Agrarian Studies
RANEPA	Russian Presidential Academy of National Economy and Public Administration
RCSD	Regional Center for Social Science and Sustainable Development
REDD+	Reducing Emissions from Deforestation and Forest Degradation
TAM	Transnational agrarian movements
TNI	Transnational Institute
UNESP	Universidade Estadual Paulista, Presidente Prudente
UNFCC	United Nations Framework Convention on Climate Change
USDA	US Department of Agriculture

CHAPTER 1
Scholars, activists, and agrarian struggles

Struggles and scholarship

Scholar-activism is a way of working that tries to change society by combining the best features of radical academic and political activist traditions, despite the many contradictions and challenges that this entails. It is not a politically neutral scholarship. In fact, it is politically biased and has its own normative assumptions. Its intellectual, political, and moral compass is the social justice struggle for a world that is more just, fairer, and kinder. It necessarily takes a bias in favour of the exploited and oppressed classes and social groups. Scholars in social sciences who claim to be neutral are often confusing neutrality with rigour. Social science scholarship can be rigorous, but it is difficult to think of how it can be politically neutral. We choose to study different social problems because we judge them to be problems. How we define problems entails some kind of social values, and addressing such problems requires normative judgements. The methods can themselves be neutral, although the choices of what methods to use are influenced by the way we have defined and framed the research, which is, in turn, normative. Our choices of analytic tools entail assumptions that influence not only the methods we use and the empirical data we gather, but also what causal relationships between factors we expect to find. So, the framing of research is a normative or activist act.[1]

In this book two types of scholar-activism are explored. One is academic work that aspires to interpret the world *and* to change it into something better, kinder, and more just, *and* where the scholar-activist unapologetically aligns with particular social movements and/or political projects. The other is activist work that aims to be more effective and carry more weight, in part through rigorous analysis and systematic research where political contention is pitched at system- and society-wide scales. For both types, theory is indispensable because it provides a logical set of conceptual lenses for making sense of the actually existing world, and it helps us to construct a normative ideal about the kind of change we want, who wins and who loses in such a change, and why and how to get there. But theory can be problematic too – unless constructed via a grounded analysis of whatever is under investigation, something which often requires historical method. Theory informs (or should inform) our political struggles, while political practice informs (or should inform) our theoretical work. The challenge is to engage with both theory and practical politics, while avoiding the pitfalls of dogmatism and empiricism. Being clear about our assumptions, normative reference points, and political stance (theory and practical politics) will help clarify our positions on some basic but important issues that differentiate the kind of scholar-activism that we identify ourselves with. For example, political commitments and intentions of aspiring scholar-activists are necessary but not sufficient to ensure the relevance and rigour of their scholarly work. But even the term 'relevance' or 'social relevance' for us is too open-ended, a catch-all phrase that can dilute what we mean by activist scholarship or scholar-activism. For instance, doing research in partnership with a big international conservation organization that practises some form of 'fortress conservation' (Brockington, 2002) funded by a fossil energy company has social relevance, but does not fit what we mean by scholar-activist work that aims to change the world towards a greater degree of social justice. Moreover, and as will be discussed later, agenda-setting among scholar-activists of different types and from various institutional bases is necessarily contested and tension-filled. The dilemmas and contradictions, tensions and synergies that emerge in the process of bringing together political intentions, scholarly work, and various (often competing) agendas is one of the thematic threads of this book.

In this book, we validate, affirm, and celebrate the method of scholar-activist work, and the role played by scholar-activists in struggles for social justice in general, and in land struggles in particular. But we do this by locating scholar-activist work at the point where scholarship and practical politics dynamically shape each other in political processes filled with contradictions, tensions, and conflicts. Stories of neat, conflict-free interaction between scholar-activists, academics, and social movements are rare; more common are the messy interactions in unruly alliances of social forces that animate the global circuits of knowledge politics and land struggles.

At present, emancipatory struggles for justice target, in various ways, the architecture of social exploitation and oppression generated by capitalism. Although capitalism is not the only powerful force at work, it is the key hegemonic system shaping global social life, including universities (Burawoy, 2014). Political struggles for justice and a better world – and, by extension, the work of scholar-activists – necessarily take place and play out within and in relation to capitalist processes. None of us can simply step outside capitalism or the material and social conditions it generates. Contemporary political struggles can be viewed as anti-capitalist when they seek to erode or dismantle capitalism and build an alternative social order.

Our understanding of scholar-activism is not universally shared. For some, scholar-activism may not necessarily entail being part of anti-capitalist social and political movements. For others, the core perspective may be anti-capitalist but not necessarily socialist. And even within the relatively narrow definition put forward above, there are variations in terms of character, scale, and direction. However, it is not a question of which type of scholar-activism is good, better, or best, but rather how one defines one's own effort in this regard. Any theory, regardless of its ideological moorings, risks being irrelevant – or worse, dangerous – to working people or those who are exploited and oppressed, if it is or becomes detached from social realities and practical politics, or is agnostic towards issues of justice. The same is true of political activism. In a dynamic world where terrains of struggle and justice change, any political activism that eschews normative reference points, without a conceptual compass, likewise risks being lost on the journey and even inflicting harm on those it claims to serve.

Scholar-activist workstreams are not the only ones trying to change scholarship and society; indeed, they probably constitute little more than a trickle among the wider communities of academics and activists. There are many radical thinkers who spawn ideas that are important for political struggles but are not committed to particular political projects or movements or the deployment of specific research methods or research protocols that are officially sanctioned by movements. There are also activists who are completely preoccupied by practical politics 'in the trenches', whose work is sufficiently informed by appropriate theories and concepts; they are found in a range of sectors, from environmental movements to trade unions. Similarly, scholar-activists' particular work and contributions are important to political work but, on balance, constitute only a small portion of the latter. This aligns with what Deslippe et al. (2016: 4) call 'the centrality of friction and an acknowledgement that academic and intellectual labour complement but never replace collective action and movement building.'

This book explores scholar-activism linked to agrarian struggles – that is, *agrarian* scholar-activism. The specific location of a given social movement within the broader productive and social reproductive sphere, as well as in relation to processes of class formation in a particular society, matters. This particularity partly determines what kind of allies are needed, for what purposes, and through what kinds of relationship. The connection between scholar-activist allies and a railway trade union struggle in New York City, for instance, will likely differ from that between scholar-activist allies and an agrarian land struggle in Myanmar. The rhythms and trajectories of those connections are likely to differ too. What kind of scholar-activism is needed, to do what, with whom, with what expectations and resources, and under what pressures – answers to these questions shape the trajectories of alliances. Our assumption is that the issue of external allies, especially intellectual allies, is complicated in the context of agrarian struggles, and especially those in the Global South. This is one of the themes explored in this book.

In this volume, the phrases 'agrarian struggles' and the more specific 'land struggles' refer to political contestations within and between the state and society, in and in relation to rural areas, and the way that political power is generated, contested, and transformed around property relations, labour regimes, income distribution, profit appropriation, and social reproduction. At present, these social processes are unevenly linked to and animated by global capitalism (Levien et al., 2018; Ye et al., 2020). As such, agrarian and rural communities are understood as socially differentiated along class and other axes of difference: race, ethnicity, caste, gender, generation, religion, and nationality, among others. Given the often highly contested and demarcated terrain in which both movements and scholar-activism seek to effect change, clarifying the location of scholar-activist efforts in relation to movements becomes imperative. Across the range of differentiated actors within movements, who are the scholar-activists mobilizing in the trenches? The answer is not obvious. In some intellectual traditions the very question itself is contested. Categorizing actors and demarcating boundaries within movements is inherently tricky and fraught; the underlying issue is a generic one about who is 'in', who is 'out', and who gets to decide. But movements are by definition dynamic and amorphous; boundaries and the identities around which they are built can be more or less fluid, porous, and malleable, at least politically speaking. Such flexibility and openness may be part of what enables movements that endure over time to change and stay relevant. So while some see scholar-activists as 'movement insiders', as a matter of course, others do not.

Gramsci posed the question more broadly: 'Are intellectuals an autonomous and independent social group, or does every social group have its own particular specialized category of intellectuals?' (1971: 3). He prefaced his answer by pointing out that 'the problem is a complex one, because of the variety of forms assumed to date by the real historical process of formation of the different categories of intellectuals' (ibid.). For Gramsci, the idea of intellectuals being 'a distinct social category independent of class is a myth' (ibid.: 1). His starting point was that 'all men are potentially intellectuals in the sense of having an intellect and using it, but not all are intellectuals by social function. Intellectuals in the functional sense fall into two groups' (ibid.). These are:

> In the first place there are the 'traditional' professional intellectuals, literary, scientific, and so on, whose position in the interstices of society has a certain inter-class aura about it but derives ultimately from past and present class relations and conceals an attachment to various historical class formations. Secondly, there are the 'organic' intellectuals, the thinking and organising element of a particular fundamental social class. These organic intellectuals are distinguished less by their profession which may be any job characteristic of their class, than by their function in directing the ideas and aspirations of the class to which they organically belong (ibid.).

Of particular concern to us here is Gramsci's note that the peasantry, despite performing an essential function in production:

> does not elaborate its own 'organic' intellectuals, nor does it 'assimilate' any stratum of 'traditional' intellectuals, although it is from the peasantry that other social groups draw many of their intellectuals and a high proportion of traditional intellectuals are of peasant origin (ibid.: 6).

Gramsci's assumption here is that once a person of peasant origin becomes an 'intellectual' (such as a lawyer), they cease to be organically linked to their original class (ibid.: 6, footnote 4). It is a controversial point and certainly open to debate.

Perhaps a good starting point for a contemporary conversation on this subject is Jess Gilbert's (2015) analysis of the 'agrarian intellectuals' of the 1930s' New Deal, partly because of the recent 'rediscovery' of the idea of a New Deal in imagining a post-pandemic world that is also dealing with the climate crisis (Patel and Goodman, 2020; Ajl, 2021; Selwyn, 2021). Gilbert argues that 'the USDA's leading agrarians were "organic intellectuals" of the midwestern family-farming class. Organic intellectuals identify with the class from which they emerge and which they serve' (Gilbert, 2015: 8). He continues: 'They create and promote an alternative understanding of reality, or counternarrative, that challenges the dominant society' (ibid.), and concludes: 'The New Deal agrarian intellectuals came from and never forgot – indeed, worked primarily for – the interest of those farm people' (ibid.). If Gilbert thinks his New Deal agrarian intellectuals qualify for the category of 'organic intellectuals', then La Via Campesina's corps of intellectuals would qualify, as would the assortment of black farmers across the United States, historical and present-day, that Monica White argues are organic intellectuals of their own class (White, 2018: 69–71). How this speaks to Gramsci's notion of organic intellectuals and the peasantry is another theme explored in this book.

As this suggests, agrarian movements are differentiated, hierarchical communities. Generally speaking, they can encompass several distinct but overlapping categories: 'cadres', who are the handful of top elite members of the leadership of movements; 'militants', who are the more numerous middle-level movement organizers and leaders; ordinary 'members', who identify formally with organizations associated with the broader movement; and the 'base', which is the amorphous community of people who, to varying degrees, are influenced by the movement (differentiating further the traditional and organic intellectual categories in Gramscian tradition). It is important to recognize this typical hierarchy of power within social justice movements, to avoid treating these movements as something homogeneous and coherent always and everywhere, and to be able to locate the origin and representation of different kinds of ideas emanating from a movement, or sections of a movement. For example, an idea claimed by a cadre to represent the movement may not always be seen as such by some ordinary movement members. It is important to recognize the hierarchy and the web of power relations that exist within and between movements, and to understand the location of movement intellectuals within it and the role that they play. This is relevant to the discussion about scholar-activists and movement relations throughout the book, because of the need to know which clusters within a movement external scholars engage with and to what extent. This crude categorization of hierarchical clusters within a movement does not stem from synthetic academic work on agrarian movement hierarchies, but is drawn from our extensive work inside agrarian movements.

Organized, structured, and overt forms of political contention are visible but not as common. Ordinary rural working people do not easily or automatically engage in overt and organized contentious politics and social movements. This conclusion is shared by competing theoretical perspectives, from James Scott's moral economy (Scott, 1976, 1985; see also Kerkvliet, 2009) to Popkin's rational peasants (Popkin, 1979). The emerging literature on scholar-activism documents and examines the relationship between activist researchers and social movements. This is important. But it brings up an additional question: what is scholar-activism and what does it do in settings and moments where, for various reasons, there is no sustained political contention and there are no organized social justice movements? In fact, it is in such settings that scholar-activist work becomes even more urgent and needed. An important assumption in the study of agrarian politics and agrarian movements is that overt political contention and agrarian movements are inherently variable, displaying diverse characteristics and following divergent trajectories across societies over time. For example, the general condition of autonomous national agrarian movements that are engaged in contentious politics is quite solid and well-developed in contemporary Colombia, in its infancy in Myanmar, and non-existent in Ethiopia. Thus, the defining commitment that we see in scholar-activism should not be talked about only in relation to existing organized agrarian movements, but also in connection with generic non-movement types of agrarian politics in which the task of scholar-activists might be to help trail-blaze the path toward movement-building. This is a significant point, especially given that this book identifies one of the defining elements of scholar-activism as being relational: if we anchor it solely in organized movements, then we preclude scholar-activism in the very settings where it is most needed.

Furthermore, scholar-activists can be based in the academy, in autonomous research organizations, or in agrarian movement organizations, and some straddle these institutional domains. There are actual and potential overlaps between movement activists and scholar-activists. Here, agrarian movement activists (cadres, militants, members, base) are differentiated from scholar-activists engaged in agrarian struggles even when some scholar-activists may consider themselves cadres, militants, or members. Put another way: cadres, militants, or members of agrarian movements are not necessarily scholar-activists; conversely, scholar-activists do not have to be cadres, militants, or members of agrarian movements even when they commit themselves to these movements.

This raises the issue of 'external allies', or simply 'allies', which – for reasons that will be explored further in various parts of this book – is a long-standing and highly contentious category of social actors linked to agrarian movements. The question of allies is raised here because, at least from the perspective of agrarian movements, scholar-activists are more generally considered part of the broader category of allies. This broad category could include any institutional or social group (such as left-wing political parties and multi-sectoral social justice movements) and individuals (including church-based actors such as priests and monks, small-town teachers, bloggers and vloggers, artists and filmmakers, and many more). Thus, for example, the Transnational Institute (TNI) is an ally to La Via Campesina (an international movement that was founded in 1993 and is mainly based among landless and poor peasants as well as small and medium farmers in both the Global South and North), as the Filipino activist painter Boy Dominguez is an ally to many agrarian movements inside and outside the Philippines (Iles, 2022). Scholar-activists form a small subset of allies. The subject of allies and what they do is important in agrarian studies and in agrarian struggles. If we consider scholar-activists to sit within a generic definition of allies, then it is relevant to briefly revisit the contested history around the question of allies and agrarian struggles; this is explored in the next section.

More broadly, social dynamics in a society in general are inherently linked to what happens in its agrarian sector, and vice versa. For example, while media spotlights might focus on debates among famous individuals and groups in key urban centres, a national political regime transition may actually be effectively decided by what happens in the rural periphery (Fox, 1990; see Franco, 2001; Coronado, 2019). This is true even in modern, highly developed countries like the United States, as partly seen in the outcomes of the 2016 presidential election, where the rural, peri-urban, and small-town constituencies supported Donald Trump (Scoones et al., 2018). Another example is the fact that ideas and practical initiatives aimed at climate change mitigation and adaptation are, in multiple and diverse ways, linked to the rural world, what resources can be extracted from it, and what waste can be dumped there (Borras et al., 2022a). Similarly, the questions of how to feed the world and how to address the chronic hunger of a billion people are challenges assigned to the agrarian sector. Historically, the uneven development of capitalism has largely rested on what contributions could be squeezed from the agricultural and rural sector, including land and labour (Wuyts, 1994; Kay, 2009). This renders agrarian struggles a strategic pillar of political struggles within and against capitalism, and the notion of 'agrarian justice' a key component of the broader concept of 'social justice'. Agrarian justice is loosely defined in critical agrarian studies as an aspirational reference point requiring a sense of the unfair treatment meted out to traditionally exploited and oppressed peoples, embedded in class and co-constitutive relations of race, ethnicity, gender, caste, generation, religion, and nationality.

*****

In this book, by scholar-activists we mean those who are engaged in agrarian struggles, committed to agrarian movements. It is thus a tiny section of progressive academic thinkers, a small section of radical activists, and a smaller section of the category of scholar-activists. However, while numerically modest, the direct and indirect impact and implications of their work have the potential to be important and far-reaching. This has always been the case, but their significance has been exponentially enhanced in the contemporary era, marked as it is by the environmental and climate crisis (Foster, 1999; Moore, 2017), the rise of regressive populism (Scoones et al., 2018), the persistence of a global food system that fails to feed a billion hungry people while mal-feeding another billion afflicted with diet-based health issues, and the status of up to a fifth of the world's working population who face precarious livelihood conditions (Weis, 2010). These factors, among others, have provoked a 'battle' for the future of smallholder farming (Patel, 2007; Weis, 2007; Schneider and Niederle, 2012; for a specifically 'generational' perspective, see Rigg et al., 2020; White, 2020). It is thus both necessary and urgent that we understand the contemporary character of and challenges to scholar-activism in relation to land struggles.

The overall narrative in this book is as follows. Despite or because of urbanization, half of the world's eight billion people still live and work in rural spaces. This rural half deserves attention in its own right. In highly developed countries such as the United States or France, the minority rural population needs to be understood, if only to explain their palpable swing to the far right under Donald Trump in the United States and Marine Le Pen in France – a swing that influences the trajectory of national politics more generally. More broadly, the rural world is key to understanding the causes, conditions, and consequences of the urbanization process. In the contemporary era, marked by all the challenges outlined above, analyzing the role that the rural world may play in any transition to a positive future becomes crucially important. But what do 'just transition' and 'positive future' mean from a rural perspective? The answer is not straightforward, and is politically contested even among progressive academics and activists. How narratives and counter-narratives are framed, by whom, and for what short- and long-term purposes does matter. Here, the role played by scholar-activists engaged in and committed to agrarian struggles becomes relevant. But this role is not straightforward either, despite popular and celebratory tendencies that suggest otherwise.

This book unashamedly and unapologetically embraces some of those tendencies. It celebrates the modest but significant contributions and accomplishments of contemporary scholar-activism in land struggles and scholarship. It affirms the importance of scholar-activism. But that is not its only purpose. More important than celebratory affirmation, this book is principally about exploring the numerous contradictions in, and difficult challenges facing, scholar-activism. It is therefore neither a glorification of the achievements of scholar-activism nor a set of prescriptive propositions on how to 'do' scholar-activism. Rather, it addresses a number of contentious issues, many of which are rarely discussed or are discussed only gingerly and awkwardly when they cannot be avoided. This book is an invitation to an open conversation about such topics, a conversation with the aim of identifying how to harness potential synergies and how to confront – not back away from – contentious and prickly issues. It does not put itself forward as an alternative to existing literature that argues for and demonstrates the relevance of scholar-activism; rather it is a complementary contribution, an effort to deepen and expand the discussion.

Historical roots of competing views on agrarian politics and allies

Contemporary debates among progressive and radical, especially anti-capitalist, activists and academics about agrarian politics and its relationship to broader class politics, as well as the role of allies, have been significantly influenced by Marx's *The Eighteenth Brumaire of Louis Bonaparte* (1968 [orig. 1852]) and the debates that it generated. One of the subjects of Marx's analysis is the political support given by France's huge population of small-holding peasants to Louis Napoleon Bonaparte, who staged a *coup d'état* in December 1851, abolishing the national parliament, gaining popular support through a referendum, and appointing himself to a 10-year term as president, with no limit on further terms. A year later he declared himself Napoleon III, Emperor of the French. Marx said: 'Bonaparte represents a class, and the most numerous class of French society at that, the *small-holding [Parzellen] peasants*' (1968: 170; original emphasis). Taking off from this observation, Marx went on to outline some of his most enduring analyses of the politics of small-holding peasants, which offer a key starting point to a conversation about contemporary scholar-activism and agrarian struggles. It is relevant to present the highlights here because of its lasting influence on activist and academic work. Moreover, it is important to reference what Marx actually said, rather than settling for the reduction of Marx's work in *The Eighteenth Brumaire* to the most popularly quoted line concerning 'peasants being like a sack of potatoes'.

For Marx, in order to understand politics, we need to understand people's location within the sphere of economic production. In his words:

> The small-holding peasants form a vast mass. The members of which live in similar conditions but without entering into manifold relations with one another. Their mode of production isolates them from one another instead of bringing them into mutual intercourse (1968: 170).

He explained that 'the isolation is increased by France's bad means of communication and by the poverty of the peasants', and that 'their field of production, the small-holding, admits of no division of labour in its cultivation, no application of science, and, therefore, no diversity of development, no variety of talent, no wealth of social relationships' (ibid.).

The character of the spheres of production, exchange, and social reproduction is central to Marx's framing of peasant politics: 'Each individual peasant family is almost self-sufficient;

it itself directly produces the major part of its consumption and thus acquires its means of life more through exchange with nature than in intercourse with society' (ibid.). He then proceeded to explain his widely influential, albeit controversial, insights:

> A small-holding, a peasant and his family; alongside them another small-holding, another peasant and another family. A few score of these make up a village, and a few score of villages make up a Département. In this way, the great mass of the French nation is formed by simple addition of homologous magnitudes, much as potatoes in a sack form a sack of potatoes. In so far as millions of families live under economic conditions of existence that separate their mode of life, their interests and their culture from those of the other classes, and put them in hostile opposition to the latter, they form a class. In so far as there is merely a local interconnection among these small-holding peasants, and the identity of their interests begets no community, no national bond and no political organization among them, they do not form a class. They are consequently incapable of enforcing their class interests in their own name, whether through a parliament or through a convention. They cannot represent themselves; they must be represented. Their representative must at the same time appear as their master, as an authority over them, as an unlimited governmental power that protects them against the other classes and sends them rain and sunshine from above. The political influence of the small-holding peasants, therefore, finds its final expression in the executive power subordinating society to itself (ibid.: 170–171).

But peasant politics in this context was not limited to the iconic conservative version described above. Marx went on to elaborate:

> But let there be no misunderstanding. The Bonaparte dynasty represents not the revolutionary, but the conservative peasant; not the peasant that strikes out beyond

the condition of his social existence, the small holding, but rather the peasant who wants to consolidate this holding, not the country folk who, linked up with the towns, want to overthrow the old order through their own energies, but on the contrary those who, in stupefied seclusion within this old order, want to see themselves and their small holdings saved and favoured by the ghost of the empire. It represents not the enlightenment, but the superstition of the peasant; not his judgement, but his prejudice; not his future, but his past (ibid.: 171).

The notion of peasant politics informed and inspired by *The Eighteenth Brumaire* is both controversial and influential. Many of the key points made by Marx will be a recurring theme in the remainder of the discussion here. There are three points that are relevant to flag at this point. First, the issue of mutually constitutive spheres of economic production and social reproduction on the one hand, and agrarian politics on the other hand, is central to a better understanding of agrarian politics. While dynamics of economic production and social reproduction do not pre-determine the character and trajectory of peasant politics, as shown in the rich and diverse literature in critical agrarian studies, it is unthinkable to have a grasp of agrarian politics where analysis is divorced from any understanding of the spheres of economic production and social reproduction. Second, the questions of class relations and class politics become central. How class relations emerge and how they are transformed into a political force – the transformation of 'class-in-itself' to 'class-for-itself' – are two inseparable social processes, politically and analytically. Third, since class is co-constituted with other axes of social difference – race, ethnicity, caste, gender, generation, religion, or nationality – our understanding of 'class agency' and class-for-itself is necessarily grounded on these mutually constitutive relations.

This brings us to an important analytical signpost about class and class consciousness advanced by E.P. Thompson, orbiting around his main point that class is relational and historical, that is, the notion of historical relationship.

Thompson argued that 'the relationship must always be embodied in real people and in a real context ... we cannot have two distinct classes, each with an independent being, and then bring them *into* relationship with each other' (Thompson 1991 [orig. 1963]: 8, original emphasis). He continued: 'class happens when some men, as a result of common experiences (inherited or shared), feel and articulate the identity of their interests as between themselves, and as against other men whose interests are different from (and usually opposed to) theirs' (ibid.: 8–9). He emphasized that:

> The class experience is largely determined by the productive relations into which men are born – or enter involuntarily. Class consciousness is the way in which these experiences are handled in cultural terms: embodied in traditions, value-systems, ideas and institutional forms. If the experience appears as determined, class consciousness does not. We can see a *logic* in the responses of similar occupational groups undergoing similar experiences, but we cannot predict any *law*. Consciousness of class arises in the same way in different times and places, but never in just the same way (ibid.: 9, original emphases).

Thompson stressed the historical dimension of class: 'these are historical questions. If we stop history at a given point, then there are no classes but simply a multitude of individuals with a multitude of experiences' (ibid.: 10). But, he elaborated:

> if we watch these men over an adequate period of social change, we observe patterns in their relationships, their ideas, and their institutions. Class is defined by men as they live their own history, and, in the end, this is only its definition' (ibid.).

He concluded that, 'we cannot understand class unless we see it as a social and cultural formation, arising from processes which can only be studied as they work themselves out over a considerable historical period' (ibid.: 10–11).

In short, it is important to clarify one's understanding of agrarian class relations, agrarian politics, and allies in order to situate discussions on scholar-activism and agrarian struggles. Without a normative understanding of class relations and class politics, there is no way for us to have a good understanding as to who wins and who loses in the social change we cause to happen with our political struggles, or who our subjective forces, reliable allies, vacillating allies, and adversaries are, and why. In turn, without clear answers to these basic questions, scholar-activists would be at a loss as to which agrarian movements or sections of an agrarian movement they should engage with and support. This is not a very original view. The long history of agrarian studies into class relations, agrarian politics, and allies reveals a sequence of affirmations of the need to embed analysis of politics in class relations, even when the latter are not the sole determinants of the former. But even old concepts such as 'allies' are not always appropriately defined or updated to address contemporary situations. For example, what does it mean to be an ally of food sovereignty movements? Even some scholar-activists are left wondering, as Duncan and colleagues (2021: 880) observed: 'Yet, the food sovereignty literature to date has not addressed the issue of how to foster such alliances or coalitions between scholar-activists and other actors in the movement'.

Historical roots of contemporary agrarian politics

Political debates about and academic research into the conditions of the agrarian world were central in social science circles for much of the twentieth century. This period was bookended by the Mexican Revolution of 1910 and the 1979 Sandinista Revolution in Nicaragua together with the 1980 political settlement that resulted in the creation of Zimbabwe. Between these events was a wide diversity of radical political projects that transformed the agrarian world, ranging from bourgeois democratic reforms to proletarian armed revolutions, from peasant-based socialist electoral victories to peasant-based national liberation wars. Some of these brought earth-shaking victories that allowed socialist revolutionaries to seize state power, as in China and Vietnam (Wolf, 1969), while others ended with peasants slaughtered in brutal military retribution, as in the case of Indonesia in 1965–1966 (White, 2016), and still others resulted in inconsequential elite concessions, superficial reforms, or even what Diskin (1989) saw as 'reforms that prevent change'. Social transformations triggered by dramatic events were not confined to rural areas. Many of these far-reaching agrarian transformations – marked by the demise of some parts of the agrarian social world, the persistence of others, and the birth of new ones – have influenced the subsequent character and trajectories of national development and political culture in a variety of societies.

At the heart of such agrarian transformations is the politics of land. This maintains or subverts patterns in the distribution of political power among social classes and groups within the state and in society, shaping the range of access to land and resources under varying types of property relations. The character of the politics of land in turn forges or refashions spheres of global social life around food, ecology, labour, citizenship, and geopolitics.

Academics have closely examined the unfolding agrarian politics of the past century. Key lines of debate have included questions about defining peasants (Wolf, 1966; Edelman, 2013) (or 'petty commodity producers' – Harriss-White, 2022), and the role of land and property in shaping peasant politics. The latter raises the issue of peasants' obsession with having a piece of land to farm, a possible source of the petit bourgeois politics of peasants. Taking off from some of the conceptual building blocks laid down by Marx in *The Eighteenth Brumaire*, the peasant political standpoint is popularly seen, at least in Marxist intellectual tradition, as permanently ambivalent towards revolutionary socialist political projects (Hobsbawm, 1973; Mintz, 1973; Lehmann, 1974; and Kay, 2002).

Heavily influenced by Marxist views, classic studies of agrarian politics have revolved around problematizing the notions of 'class-in-itself' and 'class-for-itself', with a particular preoccupation with the difficult challenge of transforming the former into the latter (see, for example, Byres, 1981). Class relations and class politics have been central in these studies. The debate as to which stratum of the peasantry could potentially be the most open to revolution has divided radical thinkers, some identifying with Wolf's 'middle peasant thesis', which assumes that the socio-economic and political autonomy of this stratum of the peasantry allows it to pursue political collective actions with fewer constraints (Wolf, 1969). The middle peasants' position of being under constant threat from the forces behind the commoditization of land, nature, and labour in the countryside contributes to radicalizing them and facilitates their move into collective action to resist the differentiating currents of capitalist intrusion into the rural areas. A competing view, put forward by Jeffrey Paige (1978), is summarized in a simple but powerful schema. Paige identifies landless proletarians, particularly migratory wage labourers working for traditional landed classes, as holding the greatest potential for the most radical and transformative – that is, socialist – revolutionary change. Gerrit Huizer (1975) dedicated much of his scholarly work to researching answers to a closely related question that defined much of this period: when and why do peasants become revolutionary (or its flipside: when and why do peasants remain conservative or reactionary)? This question has provoked a polarized, and still open, debate. James C. Scott offers a 'moral economy' perspective that focuses on peasants' resistance to capitalist forces that undermine or threaten their subsistence capacity, while Samuel Popkin advances a rival perspective from a rational choice tradition that emphasizes peasants' profit-maximizing impulses – that is, not to resist capitalism but rather to achieve insertion into it (Scott, 1976; Popkin, 1979).

Deploying a class lens in studying agrarian politics and in carrying out practical politics in agrarian settings remains imperative, but some adjustments are needed to account for the changing configurations of agrarian relations that have seen the iconic social categories of the peasant or proletariat become less common. Instead, there are fragmented agrarian classes that combine diverse ways to earn their livelihoods in the continuum between rural and urban, agricultural and industrial (Bernstein, 2006, 2010; Shivji, 2017).

Just as Marx problematized the kind of politics that the French peasants pursued in the mid-nineteenth century, so twentieth-century revolutionary thinkers have sought to understand how peasants engage in radical politics in their resolve to change their conditions, or how they become radical or revolutionary. For the first three-quarters of the twentieth century, this question was the dominant intellectual and political framework for examining large-scale collective actions of organized, structured, overt (and at times armed) defiance. Wolf (1969) and Paige (1978) are two outstanding and classic examples, while Barrington Moore Jr. (1967) has opened up a genre of agrarian studies that investigates how land politics and agrarian structures reshape the broader political institutions of societies.

Marx's take on peasant politics was a dominant influence, but not the only one, in shaping critical scholarship on agrarian politics. The long-standing and heterogeneous tradition of 'agrarian populism' is another. It can take the form of a validation of, complement to, or counter-current to the orthodox Marxist view on agrarian politics. Radical agrarian politics today, at least in its broadly anti-capitalist iterations, remains contested, academically and politically, along the continuum between an orthodox Marxist tradition, and the tradition inspired in part by the Russian populism of the second half of the nineteenth century and the views that this influenced, to varying degrees, over time (Shanin, 1983a, 1983b). Scholar-activism should be seen from and understood in the context of this analytical and political continuum.

It is relevant here to briefly revisit the historical roots of contemporary agrarian populism, as it is a tale not only of the history of populist agrarian politics, but also of some elements of agrarian scholar-activism.

In critical agrarian studies, the provenance of contemporary agrarian populism is traced to the left-wing Russian *narodniks* during the second half of the nineteenth century, who aimed to overthrow tsarist rule, resist capitalism, and rescue the surviving Russian peasant communes (*obshchina*) and their organizational structure (*mir*), which they believed could contain the seed for a possible socialist future. Narodnism ('*narod*' broadly means 'people') was a 'restorative struggle' with a tendency to romanticize communities where capitalist relations had not yet fully taken hold. Thus, the peasantry was seen as a route to socialism without having to pass through the capitalist phase of development.

It has been estimated that some 2,000–3,000 urban students went into the Russian countryside in 1874 more or less spontaneously, without any written programme or organization. These young intellectuals did not know much about peasant life or the practicality of political work. 'Moving from village to village, they distributed revolutionary pamphlets and talked indiscriminately to the peasants who crossed their path about the need to radically redistribute land and engage in revolution' (Taggart, 2000: 50). The *narodniks* would soon be frustrated by what they discovered about the peasants' politics: the peasantry did not have an appetite for revolution. The urban intellectuals imagined and expected peasants 'to be oppressed, idealistic and ripe for revolution. In practice they found the peasants to be acquisitive, conservative and profoundly suspicious of the students' (ibid.: 52). Many of these peasants would tip off the authorities about the presence of the *narodniks*. By 1877, some 1,611 of the students had been arrested. In Taggart's words: 'The summer of 1874 showed what a group of activists could do. More than that, it showed what the peasantry would not do' (ibid.: 52). The *narodniks* shifted strategy from educating the peasantry to engaging in armed struggle in the form of assassination attempts targeting the tsarist authorities, especially the tsar. Some were successful, most not. Two organizational groupings came about: *Zemlya i Volya* (Land and Freedom) and *Narodnaya Volya* (the People's Will); the latter succeeded in assassinating Tsar Alexander II in 1881.

The intellectuals in the People's Will read *Capital* and got into direct contact with Karl Marx. Vera Zasulich wrote to Marx:

> [W]e often hear it said that the rural commune is an archaic form condemned to perish by history, scientific socialism and, in short, everything above debate. Those who preach such a view call themselves your disciples *par excellence*: 'Marksists'.

She continued:

> Their strongest argument is often: 'Marx said so.' You would be doing us a very great favour if you were to set forth your ideas on the possible fate of our rural commune, and on the theory that it is historically necessary for every country in the world to pass through all the phases of capitalist production (1983: 98–99 [original 16 February 1881]).

To which Marx responded, after several lengthy draft versions of his reply:

> The analysis in *Capital* ... provides no reasons either for or against the vitality of the Russian commune. But the special study I have made of it, including a search for original source material, has convinced me that the commune is the fulcrum for social regeneration in Russia (1983: 124 [original 8 March 1881]).

The exchange between Zasulich and Marx has been the subject of much controversy and debate in the literature in Marxist agrarian studies about populism (see Shanin, 1983a; Bernstein, 2018).

While the original Russian populism was short-lived, its legacy and influence survived, partly because of its principal commitment to socialism, albeit trying to take a route via the peasantry. As Hobsbawm puts it:

> [Narodnism] is not significant for what it achieved, which was hardly anything, nor for the numbers it

mobilised, which hardly exceeded a few thousand ... [but because it] ... formed, as it were, the chemical laboratory in which all the major revolutionary ideas of the nineteenth century were tested, combined and developed into those of the twentieth century (1987: 199, cited in Bernstein 2018: 1131).

These ideas were inextricably linked to parallel and subsequent debates in Marxism: to Engels' formulation of the peasant question and Kautsky's formulation of the 'agrarian question' (Engels, 1894; Kautsky, 1988 [orig. 1899]); to Russian revolutionary ideas and practices; to Leninism and the Chayanovian socio-economic logic of the peasant economy (Lenin, 2004 [orig. 1905]; Chayanov, 1966 [orig. 1925]); and even to contemporary Marxism (see Akram-Lodhi and Kay, 2010a, 2010b; Levien et al., 2018) – all of which are relevant now in the early twenty-first century. For Shanin:

> The crux of the originality and illumination of the Russian revolutionary populist lies ... in the posing of a number of fundamental questions concerning capitalist society, its 'peripheries' and the socialist project. The attempts to disqualify those questions as belonging to the past only, i.e. representing the Russian social backwardness in the 1880s or the petit bourgeoise nature of its peasantry, have proved wrong by historical experience. The decline of peasant Russia did not make those questions disappear; quite on the contrary, most of them became increasingly global and pertinent also in super-industrial environments. Such questions left unanswered come back to haunt socialists time and time again, and will proceed to do so until faced, theoretically and politically. They can be avoided only at socialism's peril (1983b: 271).

Chayanov's theories of the peasant economy had a major influence on subsequent agrarian discourse and among key agrarian scholars such as Shanin, Scott, and van der Ploeg (see Shanin, 1971, 1972, 1973; Scott, 1976; van der Ploeg, 2013).

The extent to which the original narodnism and Chayanov have informed contemporary agrarian populism is something that, in our view, is generally assumed or theoretically extrapolated rather than demonstrated. This is especially relevant because most important *contemporary* agrarian movements do not make explicit the theoretical provenance of their political frameworks, and the few that do refer explicitly to their theoretical inspirations invoke Marx – and sometimes even Lenin – but almost never Herzen, Chernyshevsky, Chayanov or Shanin (although van der Ploeg has increasingly become an inspirational reference point to present-day agrarian movements).

It is important to clarify a central point: how did the politically loaded term 'populism' – and by extension, 'neopopulism' – originate, evolve, and come to have such a negative meaning in the Marxist academic and political tradition? In the history of some communist parties, (neo)populism was viewed from a revolutionary–counter-revolutionary (R–CR) framework. This position, held by a small but nevertheless influential section of orthodox Marxists, could – and did – lead to recurring bitter factional purges. We turn to Shanin once again for his interpretation of the history of this term, which is relevant to any discussion of contemporary agrarian scholar-activism. He explains it in the context of Marxism and the *narodniks*, demonstrating that the history of this term was intertwined with right-wing populism:

> The label 'populist', like that of 'marxist', is badly lacking in precision; the heterogeneity of both camps was considerable. In Russian speech a populist (*narodnik*) could have meant anything from a revolutionary terrorist to a philanthropic squire. What makes it worse is the fact that there are today no political heirs to claim and defend the heritage of Russian populism – political losers have few loyal kinsmen, while the victors monopolise press, cash and imagination. Lenin's major work ... from which generations of socialists learned their Russian terminology, used

'populism' as a label for a couple of writers who stood at that time on the extreme right wing of the populists ... This made Lenin's anti-populist argument of 1898 easier, while increasing the obscurity of the populist creed to his readers of today (Shanin, 1983a: 8).

Populism has become a catch-all phrase, especially amid the current rise of regressive populism (Scoones et al., 2018; McCarthy, 2019; Borras, 2020). *Agrarian* populism is conceptually plural and diverse. It is important to briefly clarify what it means in the specific field of critical agrarian studies. Terry Byres, in his 1979 classic critique of the populism espoused by Michael Lipton (1977), identified three types of agrarian populism: *classical populism*, *neopopulism*, and *liberal populism* (Byres, 1979).

Byres argued that Lipton embraces *classical populism* in as much as he has 'an almost mystical faith in the mass of the people (who happen to be rural "countryfolk") – not some of the people, but all of them who are capable ... of uniting against their urban oppressors and establishing egalitarian Utopia' (Byres, 1979: 238). He also pointed to Lipton's belief that 'the small farmer is more efficient ... than the large', as well as his holding 'a distaste for industry and a conviction that industrialisation ... is undesirable; an anti-capitalist stance; a determination to confront and reject Marxism, allied to a curious fascination with Marxist ideas ...' (ibid.).

Byres, who considered Chayanov the father of neopopulism, then argued that Lipton is a *neopopulist* because of his 'defence ... of rich peasants ... in his claim that he actually accepts the need for industrialisation, but in the distant future, and not if an efficient agriculture is possible; and in his aversion to revolution' (Byres, 1979: 238).

Finally, Byres argued that Lipton is a *liberal populist* because of his 'aversion to revolution' and 'accompanying professed faith in reformist solutions and in the power of reason and argument to secure social justice (even from dictators)' (ibid.).

Some 25 years later, Byres (2004) criticized the work of Griffin, Khan, and Ickowitz (2002) on land reform, and put forward an argument that Griffin et al. and Lipton are in fact 'neo-classical neo-populist', with their fundamentals anchored in neoclassical economics. Byres' basis for this categorization includes the position taken on social differentiation among the peasantry, the definition of class and the role of the individual, the role of rich peasants, industrialization, revolution, private property, and socialism. It is a useful heuristic tool that can help improve our understanding of the so-called agrarian populist movements active today and is particularly helpful in countering narratives that assume that the neoclassical economics version of populism is progressive, while Marxist advocacy for socialism is outdated and dogmatic.[2] It is also a reminder that while right-wing populism has to be defeated, a notion of left-wing populism may not be entirely unproblematic either, as Andrade (2020) has shown in the case of Brazil (see also Tilzey, 2019; Monjane and Bruna, 2020).

Scholar-activism cannot be taken as a homogeneous tradition, neither historically nor in the current context. When we speak of scholar-activism that is broadly located in the politics of struggles within and against capitalism, it is important to consider scholar-activism within the same dynamic entanglement between orthodox Marxist and agrarian populist tendencies. This shows contemporary scholar-activism in agrarian struggles to be, inevitably, an extension of the tensions and synergies between these two historical ideological poles that dominate agrarian scholarship and struggles. To reduce this entanglement to a straight choice between agrarian populism and class purism is intellectually and politically unproductive. The challenge is to navigate the continuum and not back away from the unresolved puzzles, imperfect political formulations, and contradictions that define it, and to find intellectual and political inspiration and energy from those puzzles and contradictions.

Evidence suggests that there is momentum and dynamism in the pluralist effort to navigate the analytical and political continuum described above. In this context, we would do well to take up the (unexpected) suggestion of a leading sceptic of contemporary agrarian movements and food sovereignty, Henry Bernstein, to go 'beyond the comfort zone of class purism' and not to dismiss today's agrarian populism. Revisiting the Russian revolution, Bernstein notes that the challenge for adherents of Marxist political economy whose strength is in socio-economic analysis is to have a better grasp of agrarian politics:

> The route from the former to the latter entails many additional determinations and complexities, as well as capacity to confront the contingent, the indeterminate and unanticipated, and to change positions, that goes far beyond the comfort zone of class purism and other illusions ... This points towards a paradox ... namely that while the best of Marxism retains its analytical superiority in addressing the class dynamics of agrarian change, for a variety of reasons agrarian populism appears a more vital ideological and political force ... In my view, the challenges facing any Marxist agrarian politics would be helped by critical engagement with the most progressive (anti-capitalist) of today's agrarian populism, and the diverse rural struggles it embraces, rather than dismissing a priori all agrarian populism as necessarily and equally 'wrong' and 'reactionary' (Bernstein, 2018: 1146).

Dovetailing with this appeal is a recent observation by Michael Levien, Michael Watts, and Yan Hairong: 'While Marxists have long criticized "populists" for ignoring capitalism and class, populists have charged Marxists with an obsessive concern with accumulation and class, an insensitivity to the contingencies of history and various blind spots regarding gender and identity' (2018: 853). They conclude:

> On the one hand, more 'populist' scholarship – whether focused on land grabs, food sovereignty or land reform – has far more explicitly incorporated Marxian insights about class and the dynamics of capitalism than ever before. On the other hand, much explicitly Marxian scholarship has moved away from its dismissal of peasant

political agency; the hyper-structuralism of modes of production debates; and linear or Eurocentric conceptions of history embedded in the transition problematic and 'doomed peasant dogma' (ibid.: 854).

This intellectual and political reciprocity does not undermine the fundamental standpoint of each camp. Teodor Shanin observed the process between the People's Will intellectuals and Marx: how each treated the other seriously and how each was willing to concede some important elements in their perspective. 'That does not make Marx into a populist or turn members of the People's Will into crypto-marxists. They were political allies, who supported and influenced each other' (Shanin 1983b: 268). Such a productive encounter in the ideological, political, and ecological terrains of agrarian movements and struggles, and those of their allies, is a key context for and object of scholar-activism on the current global agrarian front. The current configuration of our world, and how it got to this point, has partly been influenced by the historical evolution of the entanglement between orthodox Marxist and radical agrarian populist partisans.

The current conjuncture

Today, three out of four *poor* people in the world consider the countryside as the primary location of their home. Even if only for this reason, agrarian studies should remain a key pillar in social science scholarship, and agrarian politics a key pillar in social justice struggles. In many ways, agrarian studies and agrarian struggles occupy the same spaces, but not without significant changes from the past and unfolding challenges for the future. Peasant wars of the past century ended or waned as neoliberalism surged, from the beginning of the 1980s. Soon thereafter, a major context for peasant wars, namely, the Cold War, ended. Most socialist experiments collapsed, and along with them structures such as agricultural collectives and state farms (Spoor, 2008). Conventional land reform disappeared from official policy agendas, save for a few national initiatives. Promotion of market-based land reforms, land markets, formalization of private land property rights, and partial reversals of previous land reforms has dominated land policy since the 1980s (Akram-Lodhi et al., 2007; Lahiff et al., 2007; Dwyer, 2015). Academics have followed this trend in their research.[3]

During this period, as national liberation movements and communist party-led insurgencies either took state power and became institutionalized in their own contexts, or were weakened and/or decimated, different types of agrarian movements started to emerge worldwide. These are largely autonomous agrarian movements that grew in reaction to neoliberalism, and with ideological and political orientations and organizational forms that are significantly different from past national liberation movement-oriented groups. Many of these agrarian movements take some ideological inspiration from Marxism, although most are non-political party-based social movements and indeed are zealously protective of their autonomy from political parties.[4]

The emergence of these movements presents some contradictions: the movements were partly a reaction to neoliberalism (Edelman, 1999), but at the same time, they arguably benefited from neoliberalism. Such benefits took the form of the rise of the non-governmental donor complex and NGOs whose fortunes are largely a result of the neoliberalization of the global aid complex and governance agenda. These donors and NGOs in turn funnelled vast amounts of logistical and financial resources into the formation of agrarian movements that could not, or chose not to, tap such resources from political parties. The reconfiguration of political parties and agrarian movements during this period has redefined the terms of peasant alliances, with political parties increasingly relegated to the background, while NGOs and non-governmental donor agencies become more and more entrenched (Biekart and Jelsma, 1994; Borras and Franco, 2009; Edelman and Borras, 2016). It was in this context that a significant development on the global agrarian front occurred, one which would inspire deep and widespread interest and passion among the current generation of activists and researchers: the rise of transnational agrarian movements (TAMs). The term TAM is used here in a loose way to include movements, movements of movements, coalitions, and networks (for a nuanced discussion of this, see Fox, 2010).

Academic work has reflected this trend. Studies of conventional land reforms, the class configuration and class politics of agrarian movements, and their relationship to (revolutionary) political parties disappeared – apart from some serious studies of specific national phenomena, such as those in Brazil, Chiapas in Mexico, Zimbabwe's post-1997 land mobilizations, and the numerous pockets of individualized and localized upheavals among Chinese peasants whose land was being expropriated in the midst of industrial and commercial capital expansion in China.[5] In terms of research on agrarian politics and questions of peasant agency, two of the most significant aspects of this period for critical agrarian studies were the extent of and momentum behind the study and documentation of La Via Campesina, and the idea and practice of food sovereignty (Desmarais, 2007; Patel, 2009; Pimbert, 2009; Wittman et al., 2010; Mills 2021). However, this surge of intellectual energy cannot be solely claimed by agrarian studies because much work was undertaken by a range of disciplines and interests, including food, environmental, and human rights studies (see, for example, Claeys, 2015; Monsalve, 2013). And while it is compelling to look into the literature that celebrates food sovereignty, it is equally important to take seriously the sceptical views of scholars such as Agarwal (2014), Bernstein (2014), Hospes (2014), Jansen (2015), Li (2015), Henderson (2018), and Soper (2020), among others. Equally relevant are food sovereignty supporters who raise complicated and difficult issues that require deeper theorizing and empirical investigation, such as the questions of long-distance trade (Burnett and Murphy, 2014), Indigenous Peoples (Daigle, 2019), and 'localization' (Robbins, 2015).

Recently, however, there has been a convergence of sociopolitical, ecological, and economic processes in the world that has put critical agrarian studies in the spotlight. Around

2007–2008, a series of food price, fuel and energy, and financial crises exploded concurrently. This convergence was partly triggered by calls for solutions to climate change, such as biofuels, which triggered further crises in other sectors or areas, including the food sector. It was also intertwined with the rise of newer hubs of global capital (BRICS and some middle-income countries) that altered the international and regional imperatives for and patterns of agricultural production, trade, and consumption (Scoones et al., 2016). These shifts ushered in an era of renewed corporate global land grabbing instigated and largely carried out by nation states (Levien, 2013, 2018; Dell'Angelo et al., 2017).[6] They also signalled a further important change with the emergence of 'flex crops and commodities', which have multiple and flexible uses as food, feed, fuel, in industry, and as commercial goods. Crops involved include sugarcane, soya, oil palm, and corn, among others, many of which can be used for biofuels (billed as a solution to climate change), or as other food or feed commodities. While this phenomenon has affirmed the relevance of studying sectoral commodity chains or value chains, it also challenges us to trace and examine emerging 'chains of chains', or 'value webs' (Borras et al., 2016). This convergence has complicated questions of politics around (global) governance for (inter-)governmental entities and policy advocacy for activist watchdogs and social movements. And now, climate change discourse is becoming increasingly entangled with agrarian justice narratives (Borras and Franco, 2018; Franco and Borras, 2019). The intertwining of agrarian, food, and climate justice issues has provoked a similar process among the ranks of global social justice movements (Claeys and Delgado Pugley, 2017; Tramel, 2016).

These recent political developments on the global agrarian front have partly recast the units of analysis and the ways in which dynamics of social change in and in relation to the rural world are studied, as well as the object of political contestations. These transformations have generated synergies, and at the same time provoked tensions, within and between agrarian movements and other social justice-oriented movements such as food justice and food sovereignty movements, environmental justice movements, labour justice movements, and more recently, climate justice movements. These changes, including changes in land politics – materially, discursively, and politically – have far-reaching implications for how we understand and carry out *agrarian* scholar-activism today. They have also altered the character and reshaped the agenda of scholar-activism, as well as its style, methods, strategies, and tactics.

At the heart of global agrarian transformation is the changing politics of land. How we understand the problems of today's changing world helps us frame our research. How agrarian movements understand the current dynamics of agrarian transformation, especially the changing politics of land, helps them frame their political struggles. Scholar-activists have to be engaged in both processes: interpreting the world through a scholarly lens and trying to participate in the political struggles to change the world. But how scholar-activists frame research has influence on how political struggles can or should be framed; conversely, how political struggles are framed influences how research can or should be framed. We turn our discussion to the changes in the politics of land in the next chapter.

Notes

1. We thank Jesse Ribot for his input on the formulation of this opening paragraph.
2. For other recent discussions on agrarian populism, see van der Ploeg (2013), Bernstein (2018), and White (2018).
3. For a flavour of this period, see Deininger and Binswanger (1999) and de Janvry et al. (2001) for mainstream perspectives; and Zoomers and van der Haar (2000) and Akram-Lodhi et al. (2007) for critical perspectives.
4. For critical analysis and background on some of the iconic national movements, see Moyo and Yeros (2005) on international cases; Putzel (1995) and Caouette and Turner (2009) for Southeast Asia; Wolford (2010), Fernandez (2013), and Welch and Sauer (2015) on Brazil; Vergara-Camus (2014) on Brazil and Chiapas; Veltmeyer (1997)

and Petras and Veltmeyer (2001) on Latin America; Harvey (1998) on Chiapas; and Bachriadi (2010) on Indonesia.
5. For selected studies, see Wolford (2010), Carter (2015), Fernandes (2013), and Pahnke et al. (2015) on Brazil; Harvey (1998) on Chiapas (and the special issue of the *Journal of Peasant Studies* in 2005, vol. 32, issue nos. 3–4); Vergara-Camus (2014), comparing Chiapas and Brazil; Scoones (2010), Moyo (2011), and Mudimu et al. (2022) on Zimbabwe; O'Brien and Li (2006), Ho (2001), Yan and Chen (2015); Ye (2015), Yeh et al. (2013), and O'Brien and Li (2006) on China.
6. Refer to, for example: White et al. (2012) for an overview on corporate land grabs; Fairhead et al. (2012) on 'green grabbing'; Mehta et al. (2012) and Franco et al. (2013) on water-grabbing; Wolford et al. (2013) on the role of the state; Margulis et al. (2013) on global governance; Hall (2011), Moyo et al. (2012), Edelman and León (2013), and Edelman et al. (2013) on the political economy of land deals; Hall et al. (2015) on resistance to land deals; and Park and White (2017) on gender and generational dimensions.

CHAPTER 2
The politics of land

Introduction

Broad agrarian transformations are shaped by land politics; conversely, the politics of land is shaped by broader agrarian transformations. Agrarian transformations can be said to be truly global when social processes in the Global North are as compelling to examine as those in the South (van der Ploeg, 2008; Hisano et al., 2018, Magnan et al., 2022), and where the context for and object of land struggles have been altered. One outcome of this transformation is the diversification of global land issues today that have affected how land struggles are framed and pursued. This, in turn, has important implications for how we think of scholar-activism in relation to land issues and struggles.

The contemporary global land rush

The global food regime has been evolving since the collapse of the 'Second Food Regime' in the early 1970s (Friedmann and McMichael, 1989; McMichael, 2013, McMichael, 2020). Its latest changes have coincided with the convergence of multiple crises around food, energy, climate, and finance. A central theme in the current dominant narratives about the crises revolves around the assumption of mainstream economics that part of the solution to these multiple crises lies in the existence of marginal, under-utilized, empty, and available lands (Deininger, 2011[1]). The main idea is to respond to the crises by more efficiently using these types of land to produce commodities (for example, food or biofuels) via climate-smart agriculture[2], and demarcating and securing carbon sinks. This can be done purportedly without displacing local communities because these lands are assumed to be empty or under-utilized. This assumption and the associated call to action ushered in the era of contemporary global land grabbing (Cotula, 2013). While acknowledging that there are many problems in terms of processes and outcomes in large-scale land deals, mainstream thinkers believe these issues can be managed by applying 'win–win' ideas, and promoting 'business and human rights' and 'corporate social responsibility' as middle-ground strategies to expand business while respecting human rights and promoting poor people's livelihoods.[3] Hence, there has been a proliferation of voluntary corporate self-regulating initiatives such as the Roundtable for Responsible Palm Oil and many others, as well as a widespread manipulation of the spirit and intent of the Free, Prior and Informed Consent (FPIC) mechanism (Franco, 2014). Such initiatives have partly legitimized ongoing corporate and nation-state land grabbing, and have opened the door for others to follow suit in the contemporary global land rush.[4]

The land area targeted by this global land rush might actually have been larger than most estimates, probably approaching at least a quarter of a billion hectares. We have explained why this is so in our paper on the so-called 'failed land deals' (Borras et al., 2022b). It is also likely that the land rush will continue to gain momentum given the land-oriented solutions to climate change being popularly adopted in the Conference of the Parties (COP) processes of the United Nations Framework Convention on Climate Change (UNFCC) (Franco and Borras, 2021; McElwee, 2022).

Largely because of the global land rush, the wider politics of land is back in the global spotlight. The mainstream view that frames the current dynamics of global land grabbing builds on two mutually reinforcing narratives firmly anchored in neoclassical economics and new institutional economics, namely, that particular types of agrarian production systems, land uses, and land users – peasant farming, especially swidden agriculture, mobile pastoralism, and artisanal fishing – many of which encompass customary tenure arrangements (see Peters, 2022), are both economically *inefficient* and ecologically *destructive*.

Claiming that the institutions of access to and control over land and the way production is oriented and organized in peasant and pastoralist societies are economically inefficient has allowed the efficiency argument to become one of the most powerful narratives that justify, implicitly or explicitly, the contemporary global resource rush. It suggests that while the peasant and pastoralist economy may be able to help poor rural villagers to self-provision, it will not be able to feed the growing world population that has now become largely urban.

The other old but persistent claim maligns some forms of rural production systems as ecologically destructive. In the past, mainstream conservation organizations and central states launched campaigns to delegitimize and illegalize traditional practices of mobile farming, livestock raising, artisanal fishing, and forest dwelling. They deployed various schemes based on rehashed versions of sedentary farming and ranching, often using the attraction of individual private land titles to entice communities to agree. Such campaigns have resulted in livelihood disruption and displacement in rural communities from Southeast Asia to sub-Saharan Africa to Latin America. But many farming and pastoralist communities have resisted and persisted. Today, in an effort to resurrect old tactics, the mainstream narrative has found a new justification in the climate change mitigation and adaptation discourse. Shifting cultivation, for example, is framed as one of the causes of climate change, and so a method that must be stopped.

The narratives that peasant and pastoralist production is economically inefficient or ecologically destructive are powerful. Increasingly, the two are becoming fused, justifying the need to seize resources (land, water, forests) from poor rural communities (Franco and Borras, 2019; Paprocki, 2019). In the context of political claims about land, this recent development has altered the basis for redistributive land policies. Conventional land reform is based mainly on the idea of redistributing large landed estates to previously landless or near-landless peasants to create a mass of small family farms, or state farm collectives, or both, and this is largely framed as a question of economic and productive efficiency (Griffin et al., 2002).

The new context builds on conventional land reform but goes far beyond it, pushing for simultaneous land struggles under the banners of 'agrarian justice' and 'climate justice' (Newell, 2022) or even, indeed, for 'agrarian climate justice', underscoring the increasing inseparability of these struggles.

The contemporary land rush is global in the sense that it is happening in poor developing countries and in OECD countries as well as in countries such as China, Brazil, and India that are home to land grabbing corporations.[5] It also entails a wider range of natural resources – resources used by villagers not only for economic production (for example, farmland) but also for broader social reproduction.

While the land rush is largely focused on acquiring some form of land control, the logic driving it now goes beyond land-for-agriculture in the conventional sense and involves various institutional mechanisms (Borras et al., 2012) such as contract farming (Oya, 2012; Nino, 2017). Water, forests, subsoil minerals, and other resources are also being grabbed.[6] Similarly, the current land rush is no longer only about land-for-agriculture in the sense that contested lands now include non-agricultural rural lands such as Indigenous Peoples' territories and rural spaces (Moreda, 2017; Brent, 2015). These lands are coveted for a variety of purposes including housing; climate change mitigation and adaptation initiatives such as hydropower dams, wind farms, and carbon sequestration initiatives; and to meet a surging interest in urban agriculture and community green spaces (Dunlap, 2018; Stock and Birkenholtz, 2021; Torres Contreras, 2021). Some frame this current agrarian transformation within the context of extractivism.[7] Many of the issues that arise are old issues taking place in new contexts, while others are new issues cast in old contexts.

Broadening the scope of land politics

One outcome of the transformation of global land politics is that the relevance of conventional land reform has been reaffirmed, but at the same time it has shrunk in relative importance. Contemporary land issues can be clustered into four categories. Conventional land reform, which might be expressed as 'rural/agricultural in the South and North' (type I), is relevant to only one of the four categories of land politics today. In terms of academic research, this category demonstrates the relevance of political economy perspectives in agrarian studies that stress the importance of understanding dynamics of agrarian transformation brought about by capitalism's penetration of the countryside.

The remaining categories (types II, III, and IV), which arguably have always existed but were never key themes in agrarian studies, have become relevant and relatively important. The category 'rural/non-agricultural/South and North' (type II) has become, or should become, an equally compelling category for academic research and political action in the context of agrarian scholar-activism. This category is related to a wide array of climate change mitigation and adaptation initiatives and issues, notably the dramatic expansion of non-agricultural neoliberal conservation and carbon sequestration initiatives; the resurgence of hydropower projects and solar and wind farms; the massive expansion of 'no dwelling zones' in 'fragile areas' due to climatic change; and land in the broader context of social reproduction, including land for homelots, home gardens, and so on (see Shah and Lerche, 2020; Borras et al., 2021; Cousins, 2022). The sheer number of rural people directly affected by these policies and initiatives, and the logic underpinning them, require full incorporation of this category in critical agrarian studies.

The issue of rural–urban, agriculture–industry links (Kay, 2009[8]) has remained relevant, and recent developments have rendered it even more central in classical agrarian studies and critical agrarian studies (Borras, 2023; Pattenden, 2023), albeit in a significantly revised way. Recent demographic changes and patterns of capital accumulation have altered some of the traditional urban–rural links and flows including those related to land, labour, dwelling, food, water, forests, the environment, and finance. Rural and urban categories have never been as blurred, and the same can be said about the politics around rural–urban links. Moreover, and even more importantly, the rural–urban corridor has become the key site for productive and social reproductive activities of many sections of the working classes, or the 'classes of labour' (Bernstein, 2006; Pattenden, 2023; see also Borras et al., 2021). Issues surrounding the categories 'urban/agricultural/South and North' (type III) and 'urban/non-agricultural/South and North' (type IV) have thus become important in their own right as capital attempts to seize as many resources, spaces, and people as it can in order to further processes of accumulation; or where working people have brought some aspects of agrarian practices into urban spaces (McClintock, 2014; Roman-Alcalá, 2015; Jacobs, 2018; Siebert, 2020). Over the past two decades, we have seen an explosion of land conflicts worldwide that are urban/peri-urban based, involving both agricultural and non-agricultural issues.

The main antagonism in the countryside, as framed in classical agrarian studies, was that between peasants and the landowning classes (or the state, representing the landed interest) and principally centred on agriculture and broader issues of national economic development. Antagonisms rooted in land are more plural and diverse today. Landowning classes, including *latifundistas* and agribusiness plantation owners, remain entrenched and are key reactionary classes in many societies. But the current context has brought in other social forces that are equally, if not more, vicious. They include new corporate land grabbers, both transnational and domestic; cross-border non-corporate but pervasive individual land buyers such as farmers, brokers, renters, scammers, swindlers, or 'land mafia' (Sud, 2014; Levien, 2021); financial entities that include pension funds (Sauer and Leite, 2012; Clapp, 2014; Fairbairn 2014, 2020; Isakson, 2014; Visser et al., 2015; Sosa and Gras, 2021), supermarket chains and 'food empires' (van der Ploeg, 2008; Arboleda, 2020); the use of hyper-modern digital technology in land and food systems (Fraser, 2019; Carolan, 2020); an array of non-traditional agricultural investors ranging from auto companies to livestock processors (Franco et al., 2010); as well as big-time conservationists (Brockington and

Duffy, 2011; Arsel and Büscher, 2012; Büscher et al., 2012; Temudo, 2012; Pellegrini et al., 2014). Most of the lands targeted are being claimed by the central state, thus transforming the state into a big-time land broker that enables and facilitates land grabs and often deploys extra-economic coercion (Levien, 2013; Wolford et al., 2013; Andreas et al., 2020).

In settings where the land is needed but the people are not, as framed by Tania Li (2011), villagers are likely to be expelled from their land. This is especially relevant amid the rise of contemporary plantations of various types (Ito et al., 2014; Hall et al., 2017; Li and Semedi, 2021). This has inspired a surge of multi-disciplinary interest in plantation life, leading some to frame the issue from a 'plantationocene' perspective (Davis et al., 2019; Wolford, 2021; Wang and Xu, 2022). But capital is not committed to a particular mechanism or form of land control, as long as its venture generates profit. Thus, land dispossessions may be caused by market relations, alongside a variety of other mechanisms for grabbing control that often involve extra-economic coercion (Grajales, 2011; Levien, 2018), as in cases where rural villagers are not expelled from the land at all and are subsumed in the emerging capitalist enterprises. All of these dynamics have revived old and provoked new axes of political conflict, and generated a range of political reactions from below (Adnan, 2013; Borras and Franco, 2013; Hall et al., 2015; Fameree, 2016). When land deals hit the ground, they impact already socially diverse and differentiated communities. They affect different social groups in different ways, provoking political reactions that have multiple, complex, and often contradictory dynamics in terms of class and co-constitutive axes of difference: race, ethnicity, caste, gender, generation, religion, and nationality (see, for example, Gyapong, 2019).

The political dynamics in the four categories outlined above are all fundamentally about the politics of land but cannot be subsumed in the conventional land politics narratives or political agitations of the past. The social structures involved and the institutional requirements for expanding into new categories are significantly different from those associated with the conventional narratives around land politics. Hence, while old ways of asking questions are still relevant, new ones are also required.[9] Some have argued for broadening the thematic scope of critical agrarian studies to include fields that are not usually considered part of it, such as pastoralism (Scoones, 2021), migration and migrant farmworkers (Corrado et al., 2016; Delgado-Wise and Veltmeyer, 2016; Xiuhtecutli and Shattuck, 2021; Pelek, 2022), labour (Oya, 2013; Chambati, 2017; Pye, 2021), and economic production and social reproduction (Pattenden, 2018; Shah and Lerche, 2020; Cousins, 2022). While classic tools of analysis remain relevant, tools that are yet to be imagined or created are urgently needed if we are to have a better understanding of the meanings and implications of what is happening on the global land front. The majority of progressive agrarian movements frame land struggles within the conventional struggles for 'land reform', with some additional stress on 'territory' for Indigenous Peoples (Rosset, 2013). This is of fundamental importance. But even the best organized contemporary national movements remain largely focused on type I (rural/farming) issues.

If we define scholar-activism as something that is limited to engagement with organized land movements, taking its cue from these movements, then scholar-activism would at best mirror the current condition of existing agrarian movements. This would also logically mean that scholar-activism would have to contain its activities within, and content itself with, reproducing the call for conventional land reform and so also be focused mainly on type I, which is in fact the case today. Yet there are far more societies and settings where there are compelling land questions that are not politically acted upon by any social movements for various reasons, including there being no existing organized political contention and movements, or where such organized political contentions are too localized, small-scale, and isolated (Malseed, 2008). A difficult dilemma arises: what is to be done in situations where scholar-activists' work (including, for example, grounded analysis of issues, and support to frame claims and extend the reach of political mobilizations) is most needed but where there are no organized movements of the rural working classes? If scholar-activists' main entry point into grounded work is only through organized movements, then it is likely that their work will be thin in places where they are most needed. In the typology of land issues, struggles, and movements that we discussed above, it is clear that land politics has become diversified, and yet land movements have remained concentrated in type I (rural/farming). If our idea of scholar-activism/scholar-activists and land struggles/movements is an interactive one, then scholar-activists should give equal importance to settings where there are no organized movements. This means scholar-activists should work on all the six ideal-types of land politics. This is one way in which the other ideal-type situations in land issues and struggles today may be addressed amid the relatively thin presence of organized land movements in most of the places where they are most needed. We will return to this issue when we discuss 'vanguardism' and 'tailism' in scholar-activism and agrarian movements in Chapter 3.

Land movements

The changing context of land politics discussed in the previous section has far-reaching implications for the emergence of agrarian movements, the evolution of their political character, and subsequent forms and levels of movement-building and collective actions. There have been two key political transformations of agrarian movements during the past two to three decades that require brief consideration: transnationalization, and broadening of land movements.

Transnationalization

Neoliberal globalization has had, and continues to have, far-reaching impacts on working people worldwide, provoking a variety of reactions from below. For the peasantry and the rural world, these impacts have been mostly negative. This is an important context for the transnationalization of many social justice movements, including those engaged in agrarian struggles (see, for example, Keck and Sikkink, 1998; Tarrow, 2005; Baksh-Soodeen and Harcourt, 2015). While the internationalization of peasant struggles did not begin with the founding of La Via Campesina in 1993, classical agrarian studies on the politics of agrarian movements almost always focused on the local and national levels. The political dynamics between local and national politics was the central preoccupation of most studies, given the geographic and political isolation of many peasant societies from the political centres of state power, which are a key reference point for agrarian movements.

From the 1980s onwards, nation states have been squeezed from three directions by neoliberalism: from below by a widespread push for political and fiscal decentralization and administrative de-concentration; from the side by far-reaching privatization of governance structures and responsibilities; and from above by globalization and the partial surrender of significant state powers to international intergovernmental and financial institutions. Nation states and modes of governance have thus been significantly altered, but so have civil society and agrarian movements (McKeon, 2009). This has far-reaching impacts on land issues around matters related to the state and authority (Lund, 2016). Since they represent a core reference point for agrarian movements, the transformation of nation states led to the subsequent transformation of agrarian movements. Many movements have followed the same three trajectories of transformation as nation states. Some agrarian movements started to focus on subnational, local arenas of contestation, while others followed the path of privatization and became inserted into the emerging complex of state-substitution initiatives such as microfinance and self-organized irrigation associations. Others boldly crossed borders and built international networks and coalitions, but abandoned local and national fronts. Many agrarian movements vacated the national centre – but not all of them. Some attempted to establish a common political and organizational thread that would bring together movements and collective actions from the local communities to the national level and all the way to the international arena. This type of (agrarian) social movement has become vertically networked (Gaventa and Tandon, 2010). There is a similar pattern of land politics in relation to land movements, at least in terms of local and national land struggles (Lund, 2021).

The most politically coherent and significant group among these contemporary TAMs is La Via Campesina. Its mass base is diverse in terms of ideology but its global leadership has been firmly in the hands of 'radical agrarian populists' broadly inspired and informed, explicitly and implicitly, by combined sets of Marxist and Chayanovian ideas. The current leadership is deeply committed to the notion of the 'autonomy' of agrarian movements from political parties.[10] One of the global campaigns that La Via Campesina has spearheaded since the 1990s has been on agrarian reform, taken from the conventional redistributive reform framework as discussed above.

Diversification of land issues, struggles, and movements

As a result of the changed global context, social justice movements that have an interest in land issues are no longer limited to farmers' movements calling for land reform in order to establish small-scale family farms. What we are witnessing is the emergence of social movements that reflect the changing character of the politics of land and social life. Capitalist penetration of the countryside comes in diverse forms and via new mechanisms, including those that are discursively linked to climate change imperatives such as big conservation initiatives, flex crops, and commodities; and expansion of the urban and peri-urban sprawl for residential, commercial, and industrial real estate, tourism enclaves, and so on (Zoomers, 2010; Ojeda, 2012). This has in turn provoked reactions from a range of social groups and classes confronted by a variety of different land issues, which are in part manifested in the emerging political mobilizations and contentions around rural agricultural, rural non-agricultural, urban agricultural, and urban non-agricultural themes in the Global South and North.

Agrarian movements and farming

Agrarian movements rooted in and oriented towards farming in the Global South and North remain a key type of agrarian movement today. As in the past, mobilizations gravitate towards contestations over property and/or issues of production. But contemporary agrarian movements that are heavily oriented towards land reform struggles are comparatively few. There have been national agrarian movements that have made an important or even dramatic impact in their own national context and generated varying degrees of international attention and inspiration (Moyo and Yeros, 2005). The many coherently organized national land movements in this category include the Movement of Landless Workers (MST) of Brazil (Wolford, 2010) and Colombia (Coronado, 2022; Sankey, 2022); several land movements in Indonesia (Bachriadi, 2010; Lund, 2021) and India (Levien, 2018); organized and amorphous land claim makers in Zimbabwe (Moyo, 2011); and land movements using a range of claim-making strategies in the Philippines (Franco, 2008a, 2008b). There are other countries, such as South Africa (Kepe and Hall, 2018) and Ethiopia, where land has been highly contested but where the key protagonists are a combination of NGOs, development institutions, and radical academics rather than highly and coherently organized national peasant movements. There are also countries in between these two categories, which have significant levels of participation by fledgling national land movements in political contestations around land, although not as organized and well-developed. This applies, for example, to Myanmar from 2010 until the military coup in February 2021 (Ra and Ju, 2021).

Furthermore, the significant re-concentration of land in the North has triggered renewed interest and mobilizations by farmers there. In part this has been triggered by skewed subsidies for commercially powerful medium and large farms, as well as industrial food and agribusiness giants, and the inability of young and aspiring farmers to get access to land or gain entry into the agricultural sector, as highlighted in a multi-country study by European Coordination Via Campesina and TNI (Franco and Borras, 2013; van der Ploeg et al., 2015). The specific context of ex-socialist countries in the North, meanwhile, has opened up renewed debates about, and mobilizations around, land policies and agrarian movements, described by Mamonova (2015) writing on Ukraine, Visser et al. (2012) on Russia, and Magnan et al. (2022) on Canada.

Many contemporary agrarian movements have mobilized around production and trade-related issues, especially GMOs and biotechnology, corporate capture of agriculture, trade, the World Trade Organization (Bello, 2003), and the construction of alternative agricultural and food systems, and food sovereignty. A few movements, like Brazil's MST, have managed to combine land-oriented mobilizations with productivist issues. North-based farmers' organizations have been particularly active around these issues. However, while mobilizations around international trade, biotechnology/ GMOs, and the corporate capture of agriculture were particularly intense and some movements were able to use these concerns to mobilize protests in the 1990s, in recent years we have witnessed the relative waning of mass mobilizations and agitation oriented towards these matters. It remains to be seen whether the 2020–2021 farmers' protests in India prove to be an exception, or a signal for a renewed focus on these issues (Baviskar and Levien, 2021; Jodhka, 2021; Kumar, 2021; Lerche, 2021).

Furthermore, there are issues that are directly linked to agrarian matters that should be part of agrarian movements' struggles but are not sufficiently and consistently addressed. The dominant framing of agrarian reform that agrarian movements inherit from classical agrarian struggles is centrally about reforming *farmland* property relations. This is an economic production-centric framework. For us, it is a necessary but insufficient perspective in understanding land issues and land struggles today because in many, if not most, societies, land is also central to rural working people's social reproduction needs. In rural areas, in addition to access to farmland, land also means access to all, or a combination, of the following: homelots; kitchen gardens; community gardens; community forest; river, lake, or spring water; a public playground for children; spiritual grounds; a common grazing area; routes for safer and shorter journeys; and so on. The lack, or the abrupt loss or diminution of, access to all or several of these have varying degrees of negative impact on a household's ability to reproduce their labour power, and to secure the basic necessities in life: food, clothing, shelter, and care. What happens to a household's degree of access to a range of land for social reproduction will impact its ability to perform or pursue tasks in the production sphere. In fact, production and social reproduction spheres are co-constitutive (Bhattacharya, 2017; Pattenden, 2018; Shah and Lerche, 2020; O'Laughlin, 2021; Cousins, 2022). Land issues should also be understood in this manner, and so land struggles ought to be framed this way. If we draw a map of land access and livelihoods of agrarian households from a production-centric perspective with access routes graphically illustrated through lines, it will be a minimalist view: a peasant homelot and a farmland. If we draw a map of land access and livelihoods from a production *and* social reproduction perspective, it will be a complex, web-like figure. The latter will graphically show the artificial and disastrous disembedding of agrarian livelihoods from socio-agroecological embeddedness. Taking land from a combined production and social reproduction perspective means defining land access as 'a range of access to a range of land and nature' (Ribot and Peluso, 2003; Borras et al., 2021). This view allows us to better situate the issue of land in strategic undertakings such as attempts at transitioning towards agroecology (Perfecto and Vandermeer, 2010; Altieri and Toledo, 2011; Rosset and Altieri, 2017; Akram-Lodhi, 2021; Holt-Giménez et al., 2021).

Non-agricultural agrarian movements

The need in the Global South and North for rural movements rooted in the countryside whose principal interest and demands are not agricultural is perhaps one of the most significant political developments on the rural front during the past three decades. This type of movement is likely to become even more important in the era of climate change, a global resource rush, and the rise of the global precariat. As capital widens its geographic target area to secure cheap, if not free, natural resources and labour and to open up new markets, more spaces are penetrated and more people are integrated into capital-accumulation processes. Non-agricultural forms and mechanisms of capitalist intrusion into the countryside have proliferated. The most prominent of these are big conservation initiatives related to forest, fisheries, biodiversity, and wildlife; and carbon-offsetting schemes such as REDD+ (Reducing Emissions from Deforestation and Forest Degradation) and 'blue carbon'. These have been greatly strengthened politically and logistically by mainstream climate change discourses and emerging policies around mitigation and adaptation (see, for example, Corbera, 2012; Barbesgaard, 2018). Many of these big conservation projects are also heavily militarized (Dressler and Guieb, 2015; Verweijn and Marijnen, 2018). Some conventional large-scale modernist development projects are being relabelled as climate change mitigation projects; they include hydropower mega projects, alongside industrial tree plantations that have witnessed an unprecedented expansion in terms of forest cleared and area planted during the past decade or two (Hunsberger et al., 2017; Lamb and Dao, 2017; Scheidel and Work, 2018; Borras et al., 2020). There is a global trend towards rezoning and reclassifying spaces, especially in areas that are deemed fragile due to climate change, and people are being either expelled or prohibited from maintaining access to such spaces, be they land, water, or forest.

These types of capitalist penetration into the countryside have triggered the recent rise of social justice movements whose issues, demands, and struggles are not principally agricultural in nature. For example, Indigenous Peoples mobilize to defend their territory; social justice movements emerge out of anti-dam campaigns; mobilizations escalate against industrial tree monocultures; coastal communities fight enclosures that are being carried out in the name of climate change adaptation; and villagers establish movements to oppose various forms of intrusive and extractive mining explorations in their communities. Mainstream climate change discourses continue to gain momentum (Ribot, 2014, 2022; Borras et al., 2022a), framing broad concepts such as 'efficiency', 'resilience', and 'scarcity' within a neoclassical or new institutional economics perspective (Scoones et al., 2019; Vigil, 2022). We are thus likely to witness more enclosures and expulsions, as well as political mobilizations and contentions, giving rise to increasing numbers of movements that encompass a variety of land struggles, but are not strictly or classically agrarian in nature. The fusion of agrarian, environmental, and climate justice campaigns and movements is an emerging outcome of these changes in the rural front (Yaşın, 2022).

There are plenty more land issues in the countryside that are non-agrarian in nature and are rarely addressed by contemporary agrarian movements, whether in direct organizing and mobilizing work, or through coalition work with other non-agrarian movements and political groups. There are land issues related to housing for many of the rural working classes living in village centres, as well as small and medium towns, whose livelihoods are not directly linked to agrarian activities. Such people include jobless people, especially young people; street vendors; low-paid government employees such as street cleaners; low-paid casual workers in the service sectors; artisans; artisanal miners; mine and factory workers; and so on. Many of them have houses or shanties installed in spaces to which they have no security of tenure. Access to a range of land is crucial for social reproduction activities as discussed above. They have land questions, and there is urgency in their need to struggle in an organized manner to secure or maintain access to the land required for their interests. Many contemporary right-wing populists have taken up these issues and have gained support from such rural communities (Edelman, 2021; Scoones et al., 2018). But these land issues are not agricultural in nature, and should not be subsumed in agrarian movements' master frames. These issues are quite widespread given the extra-large size of the precarious rural working classes worldwide, but these are among the least attended to of rural working people's issues among organized anti-capitalist movements. Contemporary agrarian movements (and so scholar-activists) will have a role to play in terms of coalitional work with this sector.

Emerging urban agriculture-oriented initiatives and movements

As urban and peri-urban sprawl has expanded exponentially, rural and urban issues have become ever more intertwined via agriculture and industry, labour flows, and food politics; and as more agricultural lands are swallowed up by urban sprawl, more rural and agricultural spaces are included in areas officially classified as urban (Jacobs, 2018; Siebert, 2020). The reverse also applies, with urban populations spilling over into the countryside, expanding suburban/peri-urban communities, such as Russian dachas (Mamonova and Sutherland, 2015). As megacities become packed, we have seen unorganized, amorphous self-provisioning initiatives from urban dwellers in cities in the Global South and North. They plant food crops in small patches of land wherever these can be found – roadsides, the edges of railways, vacant lots – often informally and/or illegally. This runs parallel to, and at times overlaps with, a more organized and consciously orchestrated type of urban agriculture (McClintock, 2014). These emerging movements are small, scattered, often nebulous in form and spontaneous in character, but the initiatives themselves and the logic that has given birth to them constitute an interesting phenomenon that requires closer scholarly and political scrutiny because there is a possibility that this group will continue to grow and their political significance increase. All this has rendered agrarian questions even more complex to study and, on the flipside, also made examination of the urban question more complex (Brenner and Schmid, 2014).

Emerging urban non-agriculture-oriented land initiatives and movements

Finally, emerging land-oriented urban mobilizations and movements that are not agriculture-centred are worth noting. For example, urban coastal populations in many developing countries are being expelled or threatened with expulsion from their communities by governments that use climate change adaptation discourses as a pretext. Capital continues to gobble up public green spaces or potential public parks, with governments using lack of public funds as an excuse for privatizing remaining public lands or grabbing the commons and selling them to corporations. We have witnessed these trends worldwide, especially in recent decades, and we have also seen the rise of mobilizations by local communities fighting against such enclosures. These are clearly land questions in urban spaces: they are quite different from the conventional notion of the land question in agrarian studies, but they are land questions, nevertheless.

In short, during the past three decades, land politics has been transformed, and so have land struggles. Old issues have recurred in new contexts, such as the persistence of land struggles in the context of agrarian reform centred on farmland in economic production, although these struggles are much fewer and politically weaker than in the twentieth century. Meanwhile, new issues are framed in old contexts: for example, political contests around land-based climate change mitigation and adaptation measures are increasingly cast as land struggles that overlap with the conventional agrarian struggles. One of the most significant changes in global land struggles is the rise of environmental justice struggles (Peluso et al., 2008; Martinez-Alier et al., 2016; Scheidel et al., 2020). It has spilled over into the simultaneous processes of land struggles for agrarian justice and for environmental and climate justice. 'Agrarian climate justice' is the shorthand we use for this hybrid type, which may well be what defines twenty-first-century land struggles (Borras and Franco, 2018; Calmon et al., 2021; Sekine, 2021; Shah, 2022; Yaşın, 2022).[11] Activists have struggled to find ideological and political routes to navigate changes that pose existential threats to the lives and livelihoods of working people, rural and urban, worldwide. But such transformations have also brought about unprecedented political opportunities for social justice struggles. This changing context has provided a fertile ground for a surge of contemporary *agrarian* scholar-activism, and has shaped its character in terms of key actors, agendas, sites, and knowledge politics in land struggles and scholar-activism.

Notes

1. For critiques, see White et al. (2012), Wolford et al. (2013), and Montefrio and Dressler (2016).
2. For critiques, see Clapp et al. (2018), Newell and Taylor (2018), and Taylor (2018).
3. See Claeys (2015), Claeys and Edelman (2020), and Monsalve (2013) for critical insights.
4. For general critical insights on market-based voluntary corporate social responsibility schemes, see O'Laughlin (2008), de Schutter (2011), and Tsikata and Yaro (2014); for a local case study, see Thuon (2018).
5. For Europe, see the TNI report on land grabbing and land concentration (Franco and Borras, 2013) and van der Ploeg et al. (2015); see also Andreas et al. (2020) on India and China; Visser et al. (2012) on Russia; Ashwood et al. (2020) on the United States; and Xu (2019) on China.
6. On water, see Mehta et al. (2012), Woodhouse (2012), and Franco et al. (2013); on forests and green grabbing, see Benjaminsen and Bryceson (2012), and Fairhead et al. (2012); on labour, see Oya (2013); on the varying forms of land control that these all entail, see Hall et al. (2010) and Peluso and Lund (2011).
7. The literature on extractivism has seen recent explosion. For a few key ones relevant to our argument here, see Chagnon et al. (2022), Nygren et al. (2022), Burchardt

and Dietz (2014), Veltmeyer and Petras (2014), Arsel et al. (2016), McKay (2017), Alonso-Fradejas (2021), Kroger (2021), and McKay et al. (2021).
8. See also Nikulin and Trotsuk (2016) for the specific case of Russia.
9. Some relevant key studies are Deere (1995), Agarwal (1994), Bernstein and Byres (2001), Wolford (2005, 2010), Scoones (2009a, 2015), Akram-Lodhi and Kay (2010a, 2010b), Shah and Harriss-White (2011), and Moyo et al. (2013).
10. Useful historical accounts of the rise of La Via Campesina and its key features include those found in Desmarais (2007), Wittman et al. (2010), Martinez-Torres and Rosset (2010), and Edelman and Borras (2016).
11. For discussion of a similar framing, taking off from ecological Marxism and the historical case of the Dust Bowl, see Holleman (2018).

CHAPTER 3
Scholar-activism

> The philosophers have hitherto only interpreted the world in various ways, the point, however, is to change it.
>
> Karl Marx

> When I go into the classroom, or give public lectures, I try to bring to bear all the 'force of abstraction', and all the research, that I can in hopes of changing people's minds. To me, that is the true radical commitment. The irony of it, of course, is that making that commitment often requires not making better links to activists or others 'outside the academy' but, at least for a time, severing those links. Solidarity – and doing the sort of research that might just prove beneficial – sometimes requires becoming solitary. For without all that time spent in the library, at home in my study thinking, reading, and writing, I could bring no 'force of abstraction' to the struggle, and no convincing facts. So the main point bears repeating: sometimes the best way a radical scholar can 'make a difference beyond the academy', is precisely by making a commitment to doing good, radical, progressive, research in the academy. For without radical research, the chances of radical results are diminished: that is the real lesson of Marx's long hours in the British Museum, and that is the opportunity that the radical scholars who came before us have bequeathed us. This lesson, and this opportunity, should not be squandered.
>
> Don Mitchell (2004)

> I am still irreverent. I still feel the same contempt for and still reject so-called objective decisions made without passion and anger. Objectivity, like the claim that one is nonpartisan or reasonable, is usually a defensive posture used by those who fear involvement in the passions, partisanships, conflicts, and the changes that make up life; they fear life. An 'objective' decision is generally lifeless. It is academic and the word 'academic' is a synonym for 'irrelevant'.
>
> Saul Alinsky (1969: ix [orig. 1946])

Studies about scholar-activism

As explained at the beginning of this book, scholar-activists here are those who explicitly aim not only to interpret the world in a scholarly way but to change it, and who are connected to a social justice-oriented movement or political project. In the context of this book, it is about interpreting and trying to change the character, pace, and direction of agrarian transformations – at the heart of which, the object of scholar-activist research, is the politics of land – and, at the same time, trying to reinterpret and change the very institutional base of knowledge politics. In this broad sense, and in terms of their institutional base, there are three types of scholar-activists, namely: (i) scholar-activists who are primarily located in academic institutions, who do activist work and are connected to a political project or movement; (ii) scholar-activists who are mainly located in non-academic independent research institutions, who do activist work and connect with a political project or movement; and (iii) scholar-activists who are principally based in a social movement or political project and do scholar-activism from within (see related typology by Croteau, 2005: 32–35). Collectively these comprise a much smaller subset of the broader notion of 'intellectuals' in the Gramscian sense (Gramsci, 1971).

The categorization proposed and used heuristically here has been inspired in part by Edelman. In examining the relationship between academics and activists in the context of agrarian studies and activism, Edelman's approach:

> starts with an analytical distinction between three categories of people: movement activists, academic researchers in universities and similar institutions, and professional researchers in other kinds of institutions, such as non-governmental organizations (NGOs). It then argues, however, that the distinction is partly, though not entirely, a heuristic one and that the lines between activist researchers and other researchers are in practice often blurred. To make matters worse, or at least more complicated, another useful heuristic that breaks down under even minimal scrutiny is central to the way the problem here is framed. That is, the distinction between activists and researchers (of all kinds) rests to a large extent on a spurious distinction between 'doing' and 'thinking'. While such distinctions are dubious in practice, they nonetheless retain some limited analytical value inasmuch as activists and professional researchers (of both academic and other varieties) often occupy different social roles and institutional spaces and emphasize different kinds of social action (Edelman 2009: 246).

In talking of scholar-activists, the literature generally refers to academics who link up with social movements or political projects and, in the process, use those links to carry out activist academic research. As Charles Hale (2008: 3) explains, they are 'still mainly located at the margins of mainstream institutions and often prefer to speak from these locations.' A key subject of inquiry and topic for discussion in the literature is how scholar-activists emerge and survive, or even flourish, inside the academy; the tensions and synergies in their engagement with political projects and social movements; and the implications of these for both the academy and social movements. There is an implicit tendency in the literature to suggest that 'proper' academic research is, and can only be, done by academics inside the academy. Some important reflections about scholar-activism, and intellectual inquiries about activism, have been conducted by leading scholar-activists based in the academy, and some highlights of these are presented below.

Who are the contemporary scholar-activists? Frances Fox Piven (2010: 806) offers a US-centred perspective that is useful for its broader resonance. She describes scholar-activists as 'academics [who] want their work to be politically relevant ('relevant' was the code for scholar-activism in the 1970s). They see themselves as part of the political left, and they want to make a contribution to left reform efforts.' According to Piven, 'many people enter the academic world determined to become scholars because they want to be both scholars and activists.' She observes that this became a trend in the aftermath of the protest movements of the 1960s and 1970s, in which many young people had participated. She further explains that motivation comes from the idea that 'academic work can be useful in ameliorating the big problems of our society', and many academics work to influence policy (ibid.).

Meanwhile, Peters (2005: 46) argues that the regular tasks of academics, even when these are politically radical and relevant, do not make them scholar-activists. For Peters, 'Being an activist does not mean studying … someone else's struggle'. Rather, 'real activism means actually taking on an organizing challenge yourself, working collectively with others, and doing the slow, plodding, tedious work of bringing people together to make change' (ibid.). Peters' point affirms the relevance of the radical scholarship described by Mitchell (2004) but clarifies the distinctiveness of the far smaller subset of scholar-activism. Scholar-activism is a form of radical scholarship, but radical scholarship does not have to be of the scholar-activist type.

All expressions of radical scholarship inevitably bring out tension with the generally neoliberalized universities (Castree, 2000; Mitchell, 2004; Burawoy, 2014; Deere, 2018), but the tension generated by scholar-activism can also be distinct. This brings us back to Piven, who reminds us that tension arises 'when we commit ourselves to the more troubling sorts of demands that advance the interests and ideas of groups that are at the margins of public life, the people who are voiceless, degraded and exploited' (Piven, 2010: 808). She adds that this becomes even more problematic

> when we commit ourselves to the often *disorderly movements* that try to advance the political causes of these groups, when we join our critiques of the institutional arrangements that the movements are trying to change to *commitment to the movement itself* (ibid.; emphasis added).

She concludes that, 'It is this sort of divided commitment, between an academic career and dissident activism, that provokes reflection on how to do both' (ibid.).

David Meyer (2005: 193) points out the challenge of fulfilling such dual commitments, given that the two spaces of activity have different requirements, even when both demand intellectual rigour and honesty. He claims that 'one likely outcome of the separation of intellectual inquiry about political activism from activism itself is that activists or scholars who try to do both jobs at the same time do neither well.' He elaborates:

> Activism and academic study of activism become dichotomous, such that activists do not have time to think beyond the instrumental demands of the current campaign, and scholars veer into theoretical abstractions that, while potentially useful to building basic knowledge, are so far removed from often urgent contemporary questions that their works are easily ignored with no risk but to those who may have initially inspired them (ibid.).

The contribution of Hale, writing from his own experience in activist research in the context of a Nicaraguan land struggle, converges with our own take on this question. He defines activist research as a 'method through which we affirm a political alignment with an organized group of people in struggle and allow dialogue with them to shape each phase of the process' (2006: 97). For Hale, dual loyalties – to the academy and to the political struggle – are the defining characteristic of scholar-activists (ibid.: 100). He argues that:

> these dual political commitments transform our research methods directly: from the formulation of the research topic to the dissemination of results, they require collaboration, dialogue, and standards of accountability that conventional methods can, and regularly do, leave out of the equation (ibid.: 104).

Hale underscores tensions: 'Dual loyalties to an organized group in struggle and to rigorous academic analysis often are not fully compatible with one another. They stand in tension, and at times, the tension turns to outright contradiction' (ibid.: 105). But he also points out that tension does not always have to be negative. Indeed:

> such tension is often highly productive. It not only yields research outcomes that are potentially useful to the political struggle with which one is aligned; but it can also generate new insight and knowledge that challenge and transform conventional academic wisdom (ibid.: 105).

Hale concludes by coming back to the broader intellectual and political location of an activist researcher. His argument is:

> neither that activist research methods are appropriate to all academic projects nor that all innovative, radical, or transformative knowledge is produced in this way. Rather, activist research methods stand as one option among many, but they are especially appropriate to employ when an organized group in struggle is intensely concerned with the analytical question at hand and when the very conditions of their struggle involve a challenge to the existing analytic paradigms (ibid.: 108).

How can we make sense of and address the tensions and contradictions inherent in such dual loyalties? A starting point can be found in Piven's extension of the conversation, following

Alinsky, and taking a direction with which we concur. She argues that, as scholar-activists inside the academy:

> we are constantly confronted in our daily routines with the rewards and punishments doled out by our colleagues and our larger scholarly reference groups ... And every day we are surrounded by the people who will reward or punish us (Piven, 2010: 808).

When this is the prevailing condition, the pressure from inside the academy to do what 'normal' academics do becomes significant. Piven argues that we need to work to partly shape the institutional setting within which the activist commitment can flourish. She elaborates: 'we also to varying degrees choose our colleagues and reference groups, and select our associations and journals.' Furthermore, it is strategically important to consider:

> where we place ourselves in a complex ... academic world ... choosing where we place ourselves with a mind not only to the prestige of the institution, but to how it will affect our ability to do the political work to which we are committed (ibid.: 809).

The discussions of this topic by Hale, Piven, and others are important to our understanding of contemporary scholar-activism. Hale and Piven are problematizing the concept of scholar-activism in the context of scholar-activists based in academic institutions. This is, of course, relevant but it represents only one of the three types of scholar-activists mentioned above. While the other two types (those primarily based in non-academic independent research institutions, and those primarily based in social movements) are likely to be fewer in number than those based in the academy, their role is just as profoundly important and compelling politically and for the purposes of analyzing scholar-activism more broadly. The latter two categories play critical roles both in academic and activist research and in political work, and yet they are significantly undervalued and under-studied. This calls for an understanding of scholar-activists that is broader and more inclusive than the prevailing perception. Non-academy-based scholar-activists play a critical role in knowledge production and political action. They are broadly distinct from their academy-based counterparts – even when they regularly overlap with them: the boundary between the broad types of scholar-activist is blurred and porous, with regular crossover between these domains.

As a result of its emphasis on scholar-activism based in the academy, most academic literature on the subject inadvertently gives the impression that: (i) social movements and independent research institutions are one and the same; and (ii) the work done by scholar-activists based in the two non-academic sites does not have the same value or weight as the work of those who are based in the academy.

Returning to our three broad categories, scholar-activists or activist researchers can be identified in terms of their primary institutional location and their principal intellectual and political work but always in a relational and historical perspective. All three categories undertake research that is politically relevant and is engaged in political movements or projects that aim to interpret and change the world, even if their methods, traditions, and institutional constraints and opportunities are distinct. By the very definition of scholar-activism, scholar-activists in the three institutional spheres interact and influence one another; thus, they can only be understood in a relational context. Moreover, scholar-activism is a product of its own time. Scholar-activism in the context of the workers' upheaval in Europe in 1848 was very different from scholar-activism around the 1968 global student uprising, and those two past waves were different from early twenty-first-century scholar-activism.

In our experience, non-academic, independent, progressive research institutions are relatively autonomous, and many of them may have more room for manoeuvre in terms of activist research, research strategies, and in determining the political ends that research is to serve. Overall, many of them are less formal and bureaucratic, less business transactional, and less centred on individual performance, achievements, and claims. At the same time, they are also quite diverse: some are relatively conservative, politically, while others are more radical. Amongst the latter, some have provided institutional homes to public intellectuals, many of whom consciously chose to work in settings that are less constrained politically and institutionally while remaining committed to the rigour of academic research. They include some world-leading public intellectuals who have contributed greatly to the work of scholar-activism and who might be better known than many academy-based scholar-activists. Some are based more or less permanently outside the academy, while others regularly go in and out through the revolving door between the academic and independent research institutions.

This shows that significant contribution to knowledge generation that is both academically and politically compelling is not the preserve of any one type of scholar-activism, but might come from any of the three categories. Scholar-activists based at independent research organizations are often highly productive, despite having fewer resources for research, although this work is not always appropriately acknowledged and recognized.

Political autonomy and flexible funding are key features that enable these independent research institutions to carry out their agendas. It is therefore relevant to briefly discuss the various sources of funding, which have an impact on the autonomy and capacity of non-academy-based research institutions and social movements.

The first is subscription fees and regular individual donations. These provide the ideal type of funding, for the obvious reason that they allow for the greatest degree of autonomy in terms of how funds are used and for what political activist goals.

The second type, funds from non-governmental donors, which increased in the 1980s, are usually relatively flexible, politically. Much of this type of funding comes from liberal progressive or left-wing volunteer organizations that collect donations from neighbourhoods through fund-raising campaigns.

A third type of funding takes the form of government bulk funds channelled through NGOs for 'retail distribution'. This was part of the neoliberalization of development aid that started in the late 1980s, whereby portions of a country's official development aid (ODA) are channelled through NGOs which then disburse the funds to multiple partners in poorer countries. Some traditional NGOs continued their conventional fund-raising activities while tapping into government aid money for the larger portion of their total budget. This arrangement lasted for nearly three decades, but started to erode a few years ago, partly because of official austerity measures and partly as government reaction to far-right lobbies in ODA donor countries.

Funds may also come from political foundations channelled through NGOs, mainly in Europe. This is a variation of the third type, but it is worth mentioning because the size of these funds expands or contracts depending on the performance of political parties in national elections: political parties set up foundations that receive funds from government, the extent of which depends on the number of votes received or parliamentary seats won during elections.

A fifth source of possible funding is money from foundations set up by, for example, large corporations and business empires.

Finally, a further source of funding is institutions that award research grants. These have traditionally been purely academically oriented, but are increasingly opening up to non-academic research institutions, at least in the context of academic/non-academic collaborative research arrangements.

Many research institutions have a combination of these funding sources. The point is that assessing the autonomy and capacity of scholar-activist research institutions in part requires an understanding of what kind of funds they receive and from where. This, in turn, demands an understanding of the politics of the global complex of funding sources for independent research institutions, especially for those that are politically radical. While the kind of funds does not pre-determine the political character of scholar-activist research institutions, it does have some influence. The problem is that funding for politically independent (and particularly radical) research groups has been substantially reduced and continues to dwindle, especially amid the current rise of right-wing populist parties and groups in some of the key countries from which donor organizations originate (Scoones et al., 2018). Even where donors have continued to fund scholar-activist work, the terms of engagement are often politically contested and negotiated. This kind of problem is not exclusive to non-academy-based scholar-activists: those based in the academy are under constant pressure from research grant institutions, directly or indirectly, implicitly or explicitly. The challenge for scholar-activists based outside the academy is not only stable funding, but also the pressure from some types of funder and knowledge user to produce *academically rigorous outputs*, while their comrades from social movements want them to produce *politically rigorous research*. They are constantly confronted by either/or questions. Are they academics or activists? Are they part of a research institution or an advocacy group? Will they yield to pressure from the funders or to the expectations of the movements? This category of scholar-activists thus has the great privilege of having access to both social movements and academic circles, but at the same time they are pulled in two directions at once, towards either greater academic or greater political rigour.

Finally, there are some scholar-activists who are located primarily within social movements. Of the three categories of scholar-activists, they are perhaps the least distinctly recognized as such. Choudry laments that the literature on radical scholarship and scholar-activism 'rarely engages with the rich range of knowledge production from inside of social movements' (2020: 28). He elaborates:

> Indeed, much of the work on 'scholar-activism' emphasises university faculty or graduate student efforts and experiences, implications for academic careers, scholarly credibility, and implications for particular academic disciplines, rather than its use, relationship or relevance to struggles for change (ibid.).

These scholar-activists are not many in number: not for the reason that Gramsci propounded (that is, that the peasantry does not have its own organic intellectuals) but for a rather more practical major reason – there is no institutional stability, there are no programmatic plans or funds for in-house scholarly research, and no steady source of even the most minimum income for researchers.

Many of the key intellectuals within movements, especially the more senior ones, are the main dynamos behind the sharp analyses and powerful political positions attributed to the movements, but they remain anonymous. Nevertheless, while their ranks may be thin, there is almost always a core group of such in-house scholar-activists in key social movements: activists who remain committed to doing serious activist research with academic rigour in the midst of their daily work inside the movement. Some of the most influential scholar-activists in sectoral movements can be described as organic: the contemporary peasantry and their movements have thus produced their own organic intellectuals, in the Gramscian sense of the term (see also the 'popular intellectuals' frame of Baud and Rutten, 2004: 8; Tadem, 2016).

The disproportionate focus on academy-based scholar-activists in the emerging literature prevents researchers from reaching a deeper understanding of scholar-activism in general, and scholar-activism in non-academic institutions and organizations in particular. The *interplay* between the three different categories of scholar-activists is similarly under-researched and little understood. Figure 3.1 illustrates possible points and spaces of interaction. 'Interplay' can be examined from at least four perspectives: (non-)complementary engagement, non-engagement, crossover/revolving door, and presence in two or even all three sites simultaneously. It is important to probe this angle because there is good reason to believe that scholar-activists located in different institutional settings interact and engage in objective and subjective alliances in knowledge generation and political action, and we suspect that such an interaction plays a

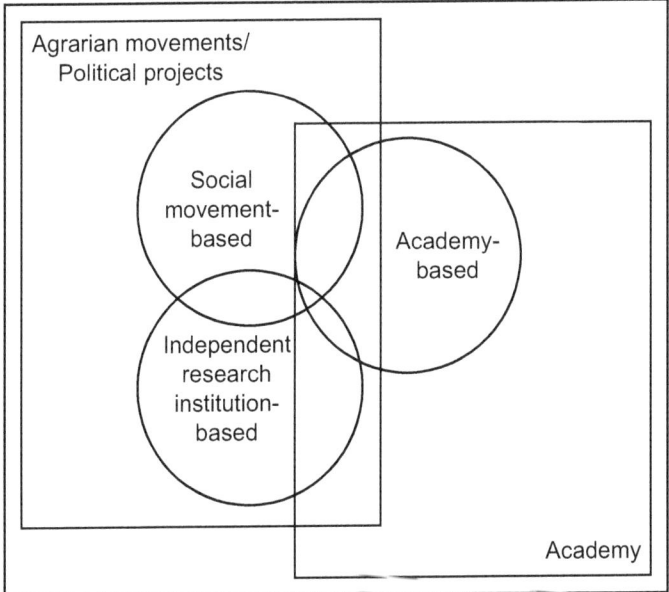

Figure 3.1 Scholar-activists in different institutional spheres

far more critical role in academic research and political work than previously recognized or acknowledged.

The discussion above brings us to the three defining elements in scholar-activism, namely, its *relational*, *historical*, and *cultural* nature.

First, scholar-activism is dynamic, and cannot be frozen as a category that sits between ideal-type activism on the one side and ideal-type academic scholarship on the other. The 'scholar-activism-ness' of a relationship between academic and activist work is a matter of degree: it could be closer to ideal-type political activism, or ideal-type academic scholarship. Defining scholar-activism thus entails specifying one's relationship with a range of institutions and actors within and outside the academy, and with fellow scholar-activists in various institutional spheres.

Second, because of the inherent fluidity of individuals, scholar-activists cannot be frozen in time within a particular category. Relying on snapshot impressions means freezing an individual into a moment, which could give an unrepresentative picture of their position on the continuum between activist and academic ideal-type poles. Scholar-activists and scholar-activism can only be recognized when seen in historical perspective and only then can they be placed on the continuum. There are excellent radical researchers who might have engaged in one research project in partnership with a radical social justice movement, for example, but this one-off engagement was never repeated. Conversely, there are long-standing scholar-activists who work as 'pure' academics for a given period, temporarily detached from the political movement, spending all their time in the library – engaged in 'abstraction' (Mitchell, 2004) – but it would be inaccurate to conclude on the basis of this period that the person is not a scholar-activist but a radical scholar. The possible combinations of activist and academic work by an individual are almost limitless.

Third, while we can relatively easily agree to a universal notion of academic scholarship, with all the caveats around colonial and de-colonial, western and non-western traditions, and disciplinary differences, it will be comparatively difficult to come up with a universal notion of what constitutes 'activist work'. The latter is in part linked to non-universal ideas of what constitutes and defines social justice movements and political contention. An ideal-type progressive agrarian movement in Latin America may look different – in terms of organizational profile, everyday political culture in movement-building, political strategies or ways of expression, and types of allies – to those in Africa, which may themselves be different to those in Asia, or those in western Europe, eastern Europe or North America, and different again to those in the Middle East and North African region, or those in China. For example, there are bound to be variations in scholar-activist work among activist academics and political activists in the broad food system (production, circulation, exchange, and consumption spheres) in the Global North. The way that guiding principles and protocols for doing scholar-activist work are interpreted and activated will differ across communities, even when they may share norms that seem to resonate universally: 'knowledge co-production', 'transparency', 'participation', and 'solidarity', for example (Brem-Wilson, 2014; Levkoe et al., 2019; Duncan et al., 2021; Levkoe, 2021; de Wit et al. 2021). The specific ways in which such guiding principles and protocols emerge and are constructed vary – for instance, between former colonial powers and the plundered colonies – and are underpinned (in that case) by colonial and postcolonial relations of power. In other words, what may be considered scholar-activism and political culture in one society may not necessarily be considered the same way in another. How political projects such as food sovereignty are thought about, constructed, and engaged in by scholar-activists in China (Day and Schneider, 2018; Yan et al., 2021), may be very different from how this is done in Brazil or the United States.

The discussion so far underscores the point raised at the beginning of this book: namely, that *agrarian* scholar-activism has inherent characteristics not found in other types of scholar-activism; and if further narrowed down to agrarian scholar-activism in the *Global South*, this becomes even more true (see, for example, the manifesto by the Collective of Agrarian Scholar-Activists in the South or CASAS[1]). This will be the main topic of the next section. Ultimately, scholar-activism can only be understood as something *inherently* relational, historical, and cultural – indeed, with some parallels to how E.P. Thompson has defined class and class consciousness.

Scholar-activism in critical agrarian studies

Our discussion now moves to a narrower section of the broadly defined scholar-activists: namely, those who work in the area of critical agrarian studies and agrarian-movement activism. We will not discuss here in detail our understanding of the field of critical agrarian studies, but our take-off point is the historization and characterization offered by Borras (2023), that is, the field as having evolved from the classical agrarian studies that had its golden era from the 1950s to the first half of the 1980s and is currently defined by its three interlocking features: politically engaged, pluralist, and internationalist.

The terms 'agrarian scholar-activists' and 'agrarian scholar-activism' will be used to refer to this subset of scholar-activists and type of work. The overwhelming majority of scholar-activists and social movements studied in the emerging literature on scholar-activism are in disciplines that are not directly related to agrarian studies, and are generally focused on peace/anti-war, labour, race, gender, and environmental themes. Studies on scholar-activism that take agrarian issues and movements as their context are not common. For reasons already explained, however, agrarian issues are key to understanding global issues; understanding *agrarian* scholar-activism is therefore key to a better understanding of scholar-activism more generally. Compared to scholar-activists working in other sectors and on other themes, scholar-activists working on critical agrarian studies and with agrarian movements may face additional challenges for a variety of reasons, including questions of 'distance' (geographic, logistical, institutional, intellectual, and political). More importantly, there are theoretical and political challenges that are distinct to the agrarian classes – as discussed in Chapter 1 in relation to the enduring views of Marx, Gramsci, and the classical agrarian populists.

As explained earlier, it is important that agrarian scholar-activism be approached in reference to agrarian movements and questions of external allies and alliances, despite – or especially because of – the limits of framing land struggles within the type I (rural/farming) category of land issues, as shown in our discussion in Chapter 2. The organization of production and social reproduction, impoverishment and drudgery, insertion into particular social structures and agrarian institutions, all conspire to impose huge constraints on and obstacles to the ability of rural villagers – especially those within the ranks of the agrarian working class and, particularly, excluded or discriminated social groups – to activate their agency to interpret and change their conditions. Hence the need for external allies who could help address such constraints on and obstacles to collective actions and, as we have also discussed, the need for scholar-activists to address issues that are outside the work parameters of existing agrarian movements.

External allies come in a variety of forms. In the last century, the most consistent allies to the peasantry and agrarian movements were revolutionary political parties – communist and socialist. Within and outside the parameters of formal alliances with political parties, there are other allies that figure in the everyday lives of rural villagers: teachers; church leaders such as priests, nuns, and monks; lawyers; doctors; and union leaders and university students who deal with complex state and corporate documents, help analyze cases and formulate petitions, provide logistics to facilitate travel to the centres of authority, or write agitation-propaganda (agitprop) materials. Many others are included and implicated in the context of allies viewed from this perspective: singers, songwriters, poets, painters, photographers, journalists, filmmakers, storytellers, novelists, playwrights, actors, theatre performers, and human rights activists. The fact that they capture conditions of and struggles by the agrarian working class, and convey these in their medium in ways and to an extent that academic or written political texts could never reach, makes these sorts of allies important.

This was the broad political context at the height of classical agrarian studies during the twentieth century, when left-wing radical intellectuals who were able to secure positions or political shelter within academic institutions and independent radical research institutions worked on questions around the revolutionary potential of the peasantry and the working class, as well as their socialist alternative politics. The era of that brand of scholar-activism ended in the 1980s.

The one thing that is similar to the scholar-activism in critical agrarian studies of the past is that the current generation includes some of the best and brightest, and most politically committed and dedicated, corps of young intellectuals. The challenges and difficulties faced by scholar-activists working inside academic institutions also remain similar to those faced by past generations of scholar-activists. Academic institutions are not always comfortable with or supportive of radical scholar-activism for various reasons, including their institutional provenance and the character and source of their funding and logistical support. Two types of institution provide particularly difficult challenges for academy-based scholar-activists: (i) institutions run by politically conservative executives, or at least those who have decided to be politically neutral in situations of great inequality and injustice in the world, which effectively means taking the side of the privileged and the oppressors; (ii) institutions run by apolitical technocrats who are guided by notions of financial productivity and efficiency, with no interest in the politics of emancipatory scholarship. The ideal setting is an institution that is committed to social justice – not just in words, but also in deed – and run by dedicated academics supported by technocrats who are at least tolerant towards, and preferably respectful and appreciative of, the work of scholar-activists. But ideal settings do not emerge from a vacuum; these are products of political contestations.

Who are the contemporary *agrarian* scholar-activists? They are a broad and diverse array of individuals, perhaps more diverse than their predecessors. They are a mixture of people across generations, academic disciplines, ideological/political persuasions, and sectoral/thematic interests, in part reflecting the kind of critical agrarian studies that have emerged today as described by Edelman and Wolford (2017) and Borras (2023). A few are veteran activists who were deeply involved in the protest movements of the 1960s and 1970s, and/or in national liberation revolutionary projects. Many of them have transitioned into contemporary scholar-activism inside or outside the academy. The bulk of current agrarian scholar-activists have emerged from post-political-party social movement initiatives of the 1980s onward, and have been recruited into, or have joined, social justice movements from different entry points, including a range of thematic and sectoral struggles and solidarity work: land struggles, Indigenous Peoples' advocacy work, or environmental advocacy organizations. An important part of the recent surge of agrarian scholar-activism comes from the food movements that have experienced great dynamism and expansion from the 1990s onwards, partly inspired and sustained by advocacy issues such as anti-GMO campaigns, advocacy for community-supported agriculture, and food sovereignty (Holt-Giménez and Shattuck, 2011). Most recently, there has been another wave of expansion of agrarian scholar-activism via the environmental and climate justice front (Martinez-Alier et al., 2016) that has revived old and inspired new advocacy issues such as agroecology. The range of academic disciplines that are being drawn in has also expanded beyond the conventional parameters of agrarian political economy to include political ecology, geography, and more, and there is now also a broader take on food political studies across world geographic regions.

The ability to transmit news and information from the countryside to the outside world, and the timing and speed of this transmission, are, and always have been, key reference points in both agrarian academic research and political activism. This is because of the 'multidimensional distance' (physical, institutional, political, and so on) of the agrarian and rural world from the centres of power, and how this impacts poor villagers' autonomy and capacity to engage in contentious politics. One of the obvious changes in the way scholar-activists carry out their work is reflected in the preferred medium of knowledge exchange and dissemination: social media. There is extensive use of the internet (further increased by the ease and affordability of setting up a website), Twitter, Facebook, Weibo, YouTube, TikTok, Instagram, audio/video conferencing platforms such as Zoom (whose popularity rose exponentially in the context of the global pandemic), WhatsApp, WeChat, Viber or Signal, texting, digital video recording and photography, GPS technology, drones, and electronic versions of publications that can easily be sent around by email.

All of these have radically altered the form of interactions among and between scholar-activists and land movements around knowledge production and exchange and political action compared to just two or three decades ago. *Speed, timing, accessibility,* and *reach* are key to the efficacy of activist research, and contemporary agrarian scholar-activists are maximizing the available communication technology in the service of scholar-activism, whether aimed at reaching the broader public or bringing research output back to agrarian movements. On many occasions, non-academy-based scholar-activists have become significantly more effective than their academy-based counterparts in terms of *popular* knowledge dissemination and in using social media as a medium of communication. By the end of 2021, TNI had more than 12,000 active subscribers for its electronic newsletter, more than 22,500 followers on Twitter, and more than 21,700 followers on Facebook; La Via Campesina had 23,300 followers on Twitter, and Friends of the Earth International 44,200. Download statistics for their publications show figures that run into the thousands for individual articles. In comparison, an author of an academic journal article could be justifiably delighted if an article was downloaded more than 500 times during a five-year period, and reached a score of ten in Altmetric (a metric tracking mention of an article in the popular media). Of course, speed, timing, and reach of scholar-activist work is one thing – the political power to make such interventions effective is another.

Scholar-activism and the academy

What are the qualities of an activist? In his classic 1971 book, *Rules for Radicals*, Alinsky outlined the key qualities of a good radical activist. These qualities include curiosity, irreverence, imagination, a sense of humour, and a vision of a better world. A radical activist community organizer, he claimed:

> detests dogma, defies any finite definition of morality, rebels against any repression of a free, open search for ideas no matter where they may lead. He is challenging, insulting, agitating, discrediting. He stirs unrest. As with all life, this is a paradox, for his irreverence is rooted in a deep reverence for the enigma of life, and an incessant search for its meaning (1971: 73).

A good activist is irreverent, subversive, and passionate. A good academic is, to our understanding, precise, respectful, and clinical. Is it possible to combine these seemingly irreconcilable defining (in our view) qualities in one person? The answer, of course, is that scholar-activists constantly strive to do just that, aiming to combine these features in their work, regardless of where they are institutionally based. These apparently contradictory sets of qualities are co-constitutive of scholar-activists: they are what define scholar-activists.[2] Scholar-activists form a subset wherever they work: a subset of academics in academic institutions, a subset of activists in activist organizations or agrarian movements. Their work is in constant danger of being dismissed as 'not academic enough/too activist' in the academy, and 'too academic/not activist enough' in social movement settings. Scholar-activists are used to not feeling fully welcome or accepted in their institutional base, of being out-of-place, an interloper. This is a permanent awkwardness, a tension or sense of incongruity experienced by scholar-activists, striving to keep their balance between their academic and activist settings.

The institutional context for academy-based scholar-activists is complex and can be harsh. In many cases, 'academic professional organizations ostracize activist scholars through a combination of self-policing censorship and the imposition of intellectual frameworks inimical to activist scholarship' (Greenwood, 2006: 319). For instance, so-called 'grey materials' – which include social movement publications, studies by independent research institutions, or NGO reports – are looked down as scientifically not rigorous. For scholar-activists working in the academy, their tasks are inherently two-dimensional: on the one hand, to link up with existing social justice movements or, where these do not exist, help build movements; and on the other hand, organize and mobilize inside the academy to effect changes in their institutional base. The university becomes the context for and object of their intellectual and political work. The complex situation is captured in a reflection by Walter

Rodney, arguably one of the key precursors for contemporary scholar-activists:

> The system will give you a nice house, a front lawn, a car, a reasonable bank balance. They will say, 'Sell your black soul.' That is the condition upon which you exist as a so-called intellectual in the society. How do we break out of this Babylonian captivity? ... I suggest first that the intellectual, the academic ... has to attack those distortions which white imperialism, white cultural imperialism, have produced in all the branches of scholarship (2019: 66).

Rodney's advocacy for the democratization and decolonization of universities is one of the key battle fronts for scholar-activists today (see, for example, de Jong et al., 2017). This further increases the challenges of dealing with the dynamics and requirements of academic work. These challenges can only be understood in relation to the need to navigate their 'dual loyalties' (Hale, 2006) or 'dual path' (Piven, 2010) and can be seen in (at least) the following areas: (i) rigour of work, (ii) impact, and (iii) reward and punishment. The research process (methods, funding and fund allocation, research questions, and so on) has been identified in most literature on scholar-activism as one of the contentious points between academics and activists pulled in the competing directions of academic and political rigour. This is not explored in detail here, but see Hale (2006), and Edelman (2009) for excellent discussions. The argument here is that such polarization is often unnecessary, and that processes and outcomes in each of these areas can be mutually beneficial to both academic *and* political work. The notions of *rigour*, *impact*, and *reward and punishment* are among the most complicated and contested concepts in scholar-activism.

Rigour

Academic research and publications have to be rigorous. This generally implies being thorough, meticulous, precise, careful, and convincing, theoretically, methodologically, and empirically. What this actually means, and what it looks like in practice, is not straightforward because it can be quite context-specific. What is straightforward, however, is the process that determines what is *academically rigorous*. There are standards arbiters including academic reviewers and review panels, editorial committees, and research councils to judge the rigour of a research grant application, manuscript for publication, and hiring or promotion processes. Key in determining what is and what is not academically rigorous is a reference group or peer reviewers who usually carry out their task in a review process. Different disciplines, institutions, publishing outlets, and journals have different traditions for determining academic rigour. They also decide whether a particular work makes a real 'contribution'. Some value fresh theoretical contributions, others privilege empirical richness. This is relatively easy for a well-trained, dedicated academic to deal with. It becomes more complicated when the dual commitments of scholar-activists come into the picture.

Political rigour is the benchmark for research as far as agrarian movements are concerned. This means being politically informed and thorough, sensitive and nuanced, and timely and relevant. It aims to understand the nature and dynamics of a social change, to understand the past in order to influence its present and future course. It is the opposite of a 'post-mortem' approach, which tends to be heavy on retrospective analysis. It means taking a position on the political processes that are being researched, which in turn runs the risk of compromising the rigour of the academic dimension of the research. Some types of militant mass movements have long-standing traditions that are not dissimilar to the academic peer review and critical self-reflection process: in Marxist-inspired movements where debates and critical scrutiny are encouraged, the principle of 'unity–struggle–unity' is aimed at achieving academic – or rather, theoretical and political – rigour. This is usually paired with the principle of 'criticism/self-criticism', which is a combination of peer review and critical self-reflection. There are arbiters of political rigour as well: the agrarian movements, specifically movement leaders, cadres, militants, rank and file; and bewildering layers of movement brokers and cheerleaders.

Isolating and satisfying the requirements for *either* academic or political rigour is the easy part. The most difficult challenge for scholar-activists, regardless of their institutional base, is how to address academic *and* political rigour simultaneously in a way that would satisfy the arbiters of both sides. But academic and political rigour may not sit well with each other, and can even be antithetical, although they can also be complementary and synergistic.

Impact

Arbiters from both paths tend to ask basic questions about the historical, conjunctural, and aspirational impact of a scholar-activist's research. There are different traditions among and between the academy and agrarian movements in terms of understanding and measuring research impact, and these can be contradictory – although they are not always. For social movements, the answer can be quite plain: making some real-life change, such as actually stopping a dam construction, redistributing land to landless and near-landless peasants, higher wages for farmworkers, or, more immediately, effectively helping social movements frame a more convincing argument and campaign. These questions around impact are important for movements and those studying these movements, especially because, as Tarrow (2005) notes, social movements often fail more than they succeed. In their pioneering book on transnational social movements, Keck and Sikkink (1998) also noted that measuring and assessing the impact of transnational social movements is complicated, but initial scanning shows that reframing discourse seems to be their biggest strength (see also McMichael, 2008, with reference to TAMs).

The academic side of the story is quite different. The evaluation of impact in academic terms largely centres on publication points, which are largely dependent on publication outlets that are ranked, in turn, mainly according to their 'impact factor', as well as the number of full-text downloads of an article. Important academic research councils that provide grants give a lot of weight to publications in academic journals with high impact factors. But nowadays, it is no longer sufficient to just get published, even in highly rated outlets. The extent to which one's publications are cited has become equally if not more important for academic arbiters. An impact tracker, the 'h-index', is a measure of the extent to which your publication has been cited by other publications.

Scholar-activists have to contend with this impact measurement requirement in one half of their two-sided world. This may not be easy for various reasons. Reacting to criticisms that activist research is simplistic, unproblematized, and under-theorized (and thus assumed to score poorly in academic impact measurements), Hale argues that 'how political commitments transform research methods and at times prioritize analytical closure over further complexity make activist research difficult to defend in an academic setting' (Hale, 2006: 101). He explains that 'activist research involves commitments that are not accountable to arbitration, evaluation, or regulation from within academia'. 'Instead', he adds, 'it requires constant mediation between these two spaces, insisting that one need not choose between them nor collapse one into the other' (ibid.: 105).

This brings us back to the question of academic and political rigour: it is not an either/or question, and if scholar-activists manage to address this dual task satisfactorily, there is no reason why they should not be seen as on a par with – or even better than – the best and brightest in the academy as measured in academic terms of research and publication impact. There are some developments that may be good news for scholar-activists. Without delving into the neoliberal logic that brought these developments into universities in the first place, three of them are described briefly below.

The first is that 'societal impact' is increasingly being given some weight inside the academy. It has different names in different settings. In the Dutch academic context, it is referred to as 'societal relevance', while in the North American context some elements of this can be included in the broad category of 'engagement'. What these terms mean is still open to interpretation. For example, an academic research project on climate change conducted in partnership with the corporate sector qualifies for societal relevance, but so does a research project that studies and at the same time politically supports Extinction Rebellion. Thus, societal relevance can easily become a catch-all phrase, and could lose its radical and emancipatory potential. Furthermore, the promotion of societal relevance in academic work can inadvertently encourage instrumentalist practices whereby academics recruit non-academic partners, such as agrarian or environmental movements or independent research institutions, because such a partnership is required in a research grant application or brings in extra points in an individual's academic performance evaluation. Such partnerships may not automatically have any political meaning. In some such cases, there have been instances where non-academic partners have been used instrumentally by the academic partner – or the other way around. Despite these various pitfalls, and the underlying neoliberal logic of this valuation system, it has the potential to provide a platform through which scholar-activists are able to collect the points they need for their academic work and, at the same time, it helps to legitimize the notion of scholar-activism within the academy.

A second development is that academic journals are now tracking an article's Altmetric score, which is a measure of the quantity and quality (different categories get different scores) of the extent to which a publication has been mentioned in the news, blogs, Twitter, Facebook, and other social media. These metrics put non-academy-based scholar-activists in a better position in terms of impact recognition than their academy-based counterparts.

A third shift is the mainstream push for open access publications. For example, the European Union now requires that the output of all research projects funded by public money must be published through open access.

These three impact-enhancing and impact-tracking systems may work in favour of scholar-activists, helping them to defend, legitimize, and entrench themselves inside the academy. There are many examples of scholar-activists based in non-academic research institutions and agrarian movements who perform better using these impact metrics than their counterparts who are based purely in the academy.

Another impact that is not easily quantifiable but is highly valued within the academy is the extent to which a publication has inspired a new generation and sparked a surge of interest in a particular research theme. Citation tracking can only partially capture this aspect. Scholar-activists tend to have a good historical record in this regard. Over the years, non-academic research institutions working on broad themes that include agrarian issues have produced some of the classics in the field that have influenced entire generations of researchers, academics, and scholar-activists. We might think of the works, both classic and contemporary, produced by scholar-activists at TNI, the Institute for Food and Development Policy/Food First, Focus on the Global South, Institute for Policy Studies, GRAIN, The Corner House, ETC Group, FIAN International, La Via Campesina, and Third World Network, among others. Not only have many of the scholar-activists in these institutions produced high-impact publications, as evidenced by statistics on internet document downloads and citations, but many of these publications have also set strategic research agendas. GRAIN's trailblazing work on global land grabs that started with a report in 2008 (GRAIN, 2008) is a good example.

Finally, scholar-activists have also played a role in redefining what societal impact means, to include not just retrospective studies, but tracking and studying moving targets in order to influence the very character and trajectory of actual policy and political processes.

Reward and punishment

Reward and punishment are powerful formal and informal norms and rules inside the academy and social movements, used partly as instruments of accountability that largely determine what scholar-activists can and cannot do. But the dilemma, as Croteau emphasizes, is that:

> work that is well rewarded within the academy may be largely irrelevant to the real-world concerns of movement activists ... [while] ...work that is grounded so as to contribute to the strategic advancement of movement efforts is not recognized as significant within the academy' (2005: 20).

Inside academic institutions, what is rewarded are works that are deemed to have academic rigour, translated into actual publication outputs that, in turn, have a significant impact based on criteria such as the h-index. Even when an institution's leadership does not agree with a scholar-activist's brand of politics, they might look the other way as long as the university can claim the productivity points. On the other hand, a performance which falls below the minimum level that academic staff are required to produce and accomplish periodically will lead to punishment. This can be swift and decisive, and can lead to jobs being lost. 'Publish or perish', a widely known informal guiding principle within the academy, is real.

Meanwhile, for the non-academy-based scholar-activist, acceptance and recognition within academic circles are probably the greatest rewards achievable from academics. Issuing an invitation to give a keynote address at a major academic conference, for example, is an important way for academics to express respect and affirmation to non-academy-based scholar-activists. This is taken seriously by the latter because acceptance and affirmation constitute legitimation of their work, and great opportunities for radical political agendas. Non-acceptance by academics of scholar-activists who are based outside the academy might be seen as a form of punishment, but more often it is just an expression and extension of the everyday elitism – which might be arrogance or, indeed, ignorance – within the academy.

For their part, agrarian movements are not in a position to reward or punish institutionally or materially, but they can and they do reward or punish *politically* in ways that are profoundly important to scholar-activists. A movement reward usually comes in the form of further and sustained access to the movement, and might even include invitations, as a guest, to a movement's 'politburo' or 'central committee' meetings. The trust that can be shown, and the openness that can be offered, are rewards like no other. Punishment happens when there has been a violation of trust, or suspicion of such a violation. Punishment is quick and complete, and almost always takes the form of abrupt suspension of access, at times expanded to broader political isolation involving other movements.

Perhaps one of the sharpest divides between scholar-activists inside the academy and those outside, especially those who are based in social movements, is that reward and punishment tend to revolve around the individual for those in the academy; in contrast, they tend to target the collective for those outside the academy. In the academy, performance and accomplishments are usually measured in individual and personal terms such as position, promotion, individual publications, individual grants, personal claims over copyright, and so on. Every unit of work expended by an individual in an academic setting is advertised and monetized, often based on formal and legal rules of work. This is in tension with left-wing radical movements, where impacts are more commonly measured in terms of the collectivity, movement, community, society, or organization, and excessive individual claims of accomplishments are frowned upon and referred to pejoratively as 'opportunism' or 'careerism'. Calling attention to and monetizing work performed by an individual tend to be discouraged.

There is of course a degree of generalization in both of these characterizations; nevertheless, there seems to be an overall pattern that demonstrates such a contrast. Academics seek to be credited for every concept they have a personal claim over that others have used, necessitating full and accurate 'individual academic referencing' for the ideas they have put into writing – even when they themselves do not always fully, honestly, and transparently acknowledge the origins of those ideas. Here is a crude example: an academic researcher studied a TAM's political advocacy campaign. In the course of conversations with the movement leaders, the academic researcher found out some less-known specifics about the strategies of the campaign, and wrote and published an article about it. Everyone who wanted to write something about the same matter, including those who might have had prior knowledge of it, or those who had gathered the data in completely different circumstances, would now be required to reference the academic researcher, that is, the 'owner' of this knowledge. Failure to reference such personalized copyright claims risks accusations of plagiarism, that is, stealing someone else's ideas. The academic researcher, whether consciously or not, appropriated knowledge from the movement, and passed it on as his or her own. As noted, this is a crude illustration, a caricature – but it does have resonance with many awkward and ethically murky situations. At the heart of this questionable attribution is the ethos of individualism in the academy.

In sharp contrast, social justice movements want individuals, other movements, and society in general to embrace and internalize the movements' ideas as their own, with no reference to individuals, but only an expectation of 'collective political referencing'. When GRAIN released what would become its massively influential report on global land grabs in 2008 (GRAIN, 2008), no individual authors asserted ownership of the ideas. When they published a reflection paper about the process and impact of their 2008 report (GRAIN, 2013), they re-emphasized the collective attribution. This is not to say that individuals are suppressed in social justice movements in favour of collective. It is simply that individualism and individual careerism tend to be generally eschewed within radical social justice movements, whereas they tend to be celebrated in the academy.

What we want to emphasize here is that there is nothing wrong with individual rewards and opportunities, whether in the academy or outside of it. However, problems can develop when this becomes the only logic or the dominant logic, and when it starts to work against a sense of the 'common good' or the broader community. Conversely, there is nothing inherently good in a collective or community framing of work, whether inside or outside the academy. Indeed, it can block the flourishing of individual agency and it is known to have encouraged free-riding. Part of what we are pointing out here is the dilemma it brings to scholar-activists who necessarily navigate both traditions. The challenge is how to strike and maintain a balance between the collective and the individual, in much the same way that E.P. Thompson and James C. Scott framed their ideas of a moral economy (Thompson, 1971; Scott, 1976): it is about the individuals, class, and collectivity all together. This brings us back once again to the three defining features of scholar-activism mentioned earlier: relational, historical, and cultural.

*****

Summarizing the discussion so far: a primary concern for any conventional academic, including a left-wing radical academic, is to examine the world in order to further enhance theories, including theories on how to change the world. A scholar-activist's principal preoccupation is to explore theories in order to enhance practical, often immediate, political work towards changing the world. Both engage with theories – with the 'force of abstraction' as explained by Mitchell (2004) – but with different starting points and end goals. This in turn defines their sense of urgency and timing. Purely academic work, including radical left-wing variants, does not compel the researcher to work with the same sense of urgency that practical politics requires, nor does it compel a rush to analytical closure that is an ever-constant pressure on scholar-activists. For example, a radical academic studying land grabbing and its implications for labour may want to wait several years for empirical data to be observable, to allow for a more theoretically robust study on how the new enterprise, built upon the grabbed land, impacts labour. In contrast, a scholar-activist is unlikely to wait for more empirical data in order to reach conclusions that are sufficient to inform intellectual and political initiatives that are aimed at immediately influencing the trajectory of land grabbing as it unfolds – for instance, to resist and oppose land grabs. This does not mean one approach is better than the other. Their rationales and their relevance are different and, while it is important to understand the differences between them, there is no point in comparing them in order to judge which is better. Neither of the approaches, on its own, can produce or represent all the knowledge that is necessary to achieve the sought-after radical social change. The key is to understand how to bundle these approaches together to collectively challenge the status quo in knowledge production, circulation, and use. In the context of anti-capitalist struggles, Wright (2019) has argued that it is not about choosing one ideal-type anti-capitalist struggle over another, but rather how to combine the various ideal-type struggles towards ultimately eroding capitalism. At an individual level, the question is not whether the scholar-activist work of TNI's Susan George is better than the radical academic work of Henry Bernstein; the question is how their works could complement one another.

Scholar-activism and political activism

In Chapter 1, the question of external allies for peasants and the social movements that represent them was explored, tracing some historical roots in Marx's *Eighteenth Brumaire* and the *Narodnaya Volya* in Russia during the second half of the nineteenth century. That peasants and agrarian movements need scholar-activists as allies was not an issue for the former. The issue was the terms of that relationship. In that context, autonomy – the extent to which external influences affect one's internal decision-making – becomes a key reference point. But it applies to both sides of the relationship: autonomy is just as important to scholar-activists as it is to agrarian movements. One-way instrumentalist relationships have marked many of the interactions between scholar-activists and agrarian movements. There are two dominant variants.

Vanguardism of scholar-activists, tailism of agrarian movements

The first is a tendency that is based on an implicit assumption that rural working people and their agrarian movements are ill-informed and have low levels of knowledge and capacity to understand and change their situation. This assumption is sometimes based on a rigorous political economy reading of the rural working people's location in the sphere of economic production. We see this in Marx's insights in *The Eighteenth Brumaire*, in which he refers to peasants being like 'potatoes in a sack', and argues that 'they cannot represent themselves and so they must be represented' (Marx, 1968 [orig. 1852]); we also see it in Gramsci's extended discussion and argument as to why 'the peasantry does not have its own public intellectuals' (Gramsci, 1971). Together with the ideological offensive waged by orthodox Marxists against the Russian populists and neopopulists and their followers, this consolidated the persistent orthodox Marxist assumption about the nature of peasants and their movements, and what they are and are not capable of achieving. Marxist critics are not the only ones to have made such assumptions about the peasantry and agrarian politics. Technocratic bourgeois liberal thinkers, especially those associated with neoclassical economics and new institutional economics, tend to have a similar perspective despite coming from a very different ideological tradition. Some scholar-activists in non-academic independent research institutions and social movements may differ little from their academy-based counterparts in this regard. In fact, it is not unheard of to see some agrarian movement 'gatekeepers' acting and talking, occasionally, like caudillos, caciques, 'chiefs', or 'petty warlords'; acting like 'masters' to peasants.

The discussion above demonstrates that so-called scholar-activists are quite diverse ideologically, and thus have differentiated views about questions of political agency and the autonomy of peasants and the movements that represent them. For some types of scholar-activists, therefore, the principal task is to do research *for* these rural poor people and their movements, and to use that knowledge to inform their political work or official policy process, thereby helping to build poor people's capacity. Knowledge generation remains primarily the domain of scholar-activists. This perspective on peasants and agrarian movements comes from a long tradition of viewing the mass of poor peasants as having insufficient agency to understand their situation and insufficient autonomy and capacity to change it. As discussed elsewhere in this book, this is part of the chequered history of many radical left intellectuals, political parties, and projects, and is one reason why post-political party agrarian movements are generally averse to 'vanguardism', or any hint of it, by scholar-activists in particular and intellectuals more generally, especially those associated with political parties.

This approach has too little faith in rural working classes, assigns a subordinate role to agrarian movements, and accords scholar-activists a vanguard role in terms of knowledge generation. In this tradition, agrarian movements are essentially treated as adjunct to the intellectual and/or political agenda/project of scholar-activists, and many movements, for various reasons, tend to be compliant. The extreme version of this tendency then is a dual problem of vanguardism by scholar-activists and tailism by agrarian movements. Thus, we see high-profile agrarian movement organizations in which a handful of vanguards (almost always the intellectuals, scholar-activists, and gatekeepers, or the leading political parties) make all the noise and claim representation, while the mass base has long been demobilized and become dormant.

Tailism of scholar-activists, vanguardism of agrarian movements

The second variant – the opposite of the first, and perhaps a reaction to it on some occasions – is a tendency for agrarian movements to set the agenda and scholar-activists to simply follow. This variant is based on the romanticized idea that everything that agrarian movements say and do is good and correct, and should be supported unconditionally by scholar-activists. It is arguably a kind of 'mass line', in Maoist terms, taken to extremes or deployed out of context. Let us recall what Mao said: 'The masses are the real heroes, while we ourselves are often childish and ignorant, and without this understanding, it is impossible to acquire even the most rudimentary knowledge' (Mao, 1975: 12). This out-of-context, romanticized version of the mass line demonstrates a rather naive understanding of the political dynamics and actual workings of agrarian movements.

Looking more generally at the relationship between scholars, the left, and movements, Lemisch summarized some of the contradictions and dilemmas related to our discussion point:

> But letting a movement define your scholarly goals and the questions that you ask isn't good for the left. A vital source of debate and criticism will be cut off if the left's intellectuals become captives of a current left and reduce themselves to ... a merely 'accompanying' role ... For an intellectual, mere accompaniment is an abandonment of the historian's critical responsibility ... We don't serve the people very well by uncritical admiration (2004: 193).

Returning to the specifics of agrarian scholar-activism, we might ask: in settings where there are no overt political contentions and organized movements, what then would scholar-activism mean? To merely accompany the poor, document and write about their condition? Or does it mean more than that, even to the point of digging the trenches and working in them in order to directly help build a movement, for instance? In settings where there are organized groups, the inner workings of agrarian movements are not only far from perfect, but are power-ridden processes, at times manipulated and constantly contested by competing actors and factions within and from outside the movements. Representation is not always democratic, and internal accountability not always a strong point in agrarian movements – or any political movement for that matter. Mendez shares what she has seen inside organizations and offers words of caution to scholar-activists:

> Scholar-activists should be careful not to presuppose a Pollyanna view of poor, guileless, local organizations incapable of 'using' the scholar-activist or research projects to further particular individual, political, or small-group agendas. We should not assume some kind of rosy, romantic relationship between scholar-activists and 'local' organizations. In an age of globalization we should also be wary of romanticizing local communities as the repositories of 'authentic, local truths'. Communities and organizations are not homogenous, nor are they free from internal conflict, power struggles, and contradictions ... It is virtually impossible for the scholar-activist to assume the position of neutral observer when it comes to these internal conflicts (2006: 153).

Taking at face value what the movement leaders say or show often leads scholar-activists to write about or support processes that are not deserving of support, or else results in the failure to support deserving causes. Scholar-activists in this mould tend to reinforce the problematic leadership of caudillo-cum-cacique type leaders, or strengthen and legitimize problematic roles played by undemocratic and even despotic movement brokers, or support problematic political positions. They inadvertently dismiss fascinating movements and collective actions just because they do not have leaders who are able to express and amplify important accomplishments, and may instead pick up on movements that are actually empty shells simply because these have eloquent elite leaders, or leaders who pay their way to meetings and conferences in the national capital or abroad. Edelman cautions us about:

> the activists' investment in presenting overly coherent 'official narratives' about their movements and in making representation claims that may or may not have a solid basis. At times academic researchers and other professional intellectuals knowingly or

unknowingly collude in producing and propagating those narratives and in 'airbrushing' (or, to be more up-to-date, 'photo-shopping') out dimensions of activists' biographies and of social movement practice that conflict with or complicate the 'official' picture or line. Whether or not this cosmetic approach, which in its more extreme manifestations critics sometimes characterize as 'self-censorship', 'uncritical adulation' or even 'cheerleading', really serves the needs of social movements is an important question (2009: 249).

Moreover, it is not uncommon for a rich peasant organization to generate popular support by claiming to represent all peasants: small, medium and big. In this situation the worst scenario is the presence of a triangular reinforcing interaction between caudillo agrarian movement leaders (who promote often empty movements or rich peasant movements claiming representation of all 'people of the land'); layers of movement brokers and cheerleaders (many of whom could be romantic and/or impetuous petit bourgeois intellectuals); and uncritical scholar-activists (especially those who do not deploy rigorous class analysis), who take the grand claims by movement leaders, brokers, and cheerleaders at face value. In this context, a celebrated and romanticized vanguard role is being accorded to agrarian movements, and a subordinate role to scholar-activists. Here, scholar-activists are relegated to the role of adjunct to the political and logistical agenda of the agrarian movements, and quietly acquiesce to this demotion. The extreme version of this tendency is a dual problem of vanguardism of agrarian movements and tailism of scholar-activists.

Interactive scholar-activist and agrarian movement engagement

Both the dominant tendencies discussed above are instrumentalist and problematic. We need a third approach that is a two-way, mutually reinforcing, interactive approach to agrarian movement and scholar-activist relationships. On the one hand, this approach values the expertise of scholar-activists in helping agrarian movements to overcome constraints and obstacles to, and to extend the reach of, their political struggles. On the other hand, this approach values the autonomy of agrarian movements in the conduct of their movement-building and collective actions. Realizing that there is great potential for synergies in joining forces, scholar-activists and agrarian movements can forge a rewarding alliance. These are some of the fundamental assumptions, more or less, of some of the pioneers of participatory action research such as the Colombian sociologist Orlando Fals Borda (Rappaport, 2020). As Edelman explains, 'some important synergies between social movements and academics could involve exchanges of knowledge and contacts, joint strategy discussions, publicizing organizations' platforms and activities and analyzing their histories, and engaging in collaborative research and training' (2009: 247). An important starting point for such an approach is an honest and objective understanding of where each party is coming from and their motivations for the interaction. It is an approach that recognizes the autonomy of both parties, and therefore negotiates the terms of their engagement. It is an approach that recognizes the capacity of agrarian movements and scholar-activists to generate knowledge, albeit in different ways, and understands that such knowledge can be more powerful when pooled.

The two sets of actors have different provenances and different institutional starting points and interests in generating knowledge and engaging in political struggles. This becomes even more complicated when seen from a disaggregated perspective on scholar-activists. For example, scholar-activists might be thinking of theorizing food sovereignty as an alternative food system, while a local agrarian movement organization may be interested in an immediate issue such as linking up with public free school meal programmes. Or it may be the opposite: scholar-activists may be interested only in concluding a one-year research project and getting some journal articles published, while agrarian movements may be thinking of a larger goal such as a society-wide land redistribution programme. These different starting points and institutional interests mean that engagements between agrarian movements and scholar-activists are inherently filled with both potential and tension, as well as actual conflict.

Croteau et al. explain that 'both social movements theorists and movement activists are located in structural systems that create constraints on our efforts as well as provide possibilities for action' (2005: xv–xvi). They further argue that 'The tension between theory and practice needs to be understood in relation to larger structural forces rather than being individualized as the problem or vision of a single academic or activist' (ibid.). As Routledge and Derickson remind us, scholar-activists identify and side with 'struggles of marginalized communities in ways that reject, but do not ignore, the violent and imperialist histories of the academy' (2015: 391). For Fox, the two parties are in the best position 'to find positive synergy between the needs of activist partners and the empirical and analytical rigour of scholarship if [they] recognize the tensions between the forces that shape the two sets of agendas' (2006: 30). Studying agrarian movements in Latin America, Edelman explains that 'tensions between activists and academics ... tend to revolve more narrowly around the research process and the purpose and methods of knowledge production and dissemination' (2009: 247). Such differences are not insurmountable. As Fox reminds us, 'Activist–scholar partnerships, if they are to work, need to be based on an understanding of the other, respect for difference, shared tractable goals, and a willingness to agree to disagree' (2006: 31). He concludes that:

> Ideas like partnership and coalition – more than the term solidarity, for example – recognize that the participants are autonomous actors that each bring their/our own agendas, priorities, and – whether we recognize it or not – baggage to the table. Coalitions and partnerships that last are grounded in more than shared values, but in shared interests as well (ibid.: 32).

Exploring the politics of sustainability of development, Ian Scoones underscored similar tensions, and described the messy interaction among those engaged in knowledge politics. He explained that 'Transformations to sustainability and development cannot be ordered, managed, and controlled, but must emerge from unruly political alliances, diverse knowledges, and collective organization' (Scoones 2016: 308). A two-way, mutually reinforcing approach to scholar-activist/agrarian movement relationships necessarily leads to a mutual internalization of passions and contradictions of both sets of actors. Reflecting on his involvement with land struggles in Nicaragua, Hale says:

> These movements are both inspiring and compromised; movement activists are courageous advocates of local and global justice yet partly implicated in the very systems of oppression they set out to oppose. My argument takes shape by viewing these two lines of inquiry through a single lens. To align oneself with a political struggle while carrying out research on issues related to that struggle is to occupy a space of profoundly generative scholarly understanding. Yet when we position ourselves in such spaces, we are also inevitably drawn into the compromised conditions of the political process. The resulting contradictions make the research more difficult to carry out, but they also generate insight that otherwise would be impossible to achieve. This insight, in turn, provides an often unacknowledged basis for analytical understanding and theoretical innovation (2006: 98).

In short, scholar-activists and agrarian movements emerge autonomously from each other. In the process of pursuing their own trajectories, they get entangled with one another. This relationship manifests in diverse ways, and can assume less productive and even problematic types. A mutually reinforcing, interactive relationship between the two leads to messy dynamics of engagement, but holds the greatest potential in terms of producing progressive change in societies.

Nevertheless, while we recognize high degrees of political agency among scholar-activists and agrarian movements, they carry out their scholarly and political work in circumstances not of their own choosing, in conditions that are difficult and even hostile. In Chapter 4, we discuss the other difficult challenges in pursuing scholar-activism.

Notes

1. See <https://casasouth.org/sample-page/> [accessed 3 April 2023]
2. See also Martinez-Alier et al. (2011) in the context of environmental justice activism and scholarship.

CHAPTER 4
What is to be done? Future challenges for agrarian scholar-activism

Ian Scoones examined the politics of the International Assessment of Agricultural Knowledge, Science and Technology for Development (IAASTD) and concluded:

> some of the knowledge contests involved in the assessment ... illuminate four questions at the heart of contemporary democratic theory and practice: how do processes of knowledge framing occur; how do different practices and methodologies get deployed in cross-cultural, global processes; how is 'representation' constructed and legitimised; and how, as a result, do collective understandings of global issues emerge? ... in assessments of this sort, the politics of knowledge needs to be made more explicit, and negotiations around politics and values, framings and perspectives, need to be put centre-stage in assessment design (2009b: 547).

The politics of knowledge are played out in, among other sites, the competing interpretations of the world and how to change it. The fiercely contested knowledge politics flagged by Scoones when drawing on the IAASTD experience more than a decade ago are now playing out in similar ways in the climate change debate. Jesse Ribot has spotlighted such dynamics of knowledge politics:

> Predominant and ostensibly scientific frames for evaluating climate-related loss and damage focus on the climate events as the primary cause. This approach

> clouds out and silences the many non-climatic, social and political-economic, causes of crises. Framing the social back in highlights a fuller range of causes and potential solutions. It is also contentious as it locates cause in decisions, policies and institutions – indicating responsibility and blame. Choosing a social and political-economic analytic has implications for action and ethics as it broadens response abilities and responsibility (2022: 683).

Scholar-activism is centrally about contesting dominant but flawed assumptions about social problems such as climate change. But as Scoones and Ribot remind us, there are diverse and competing voices and frames: which voices are heard and frames adopted, and why? The highly undemocratic and neocolonial global circuits of knowledge reinforce, amplify, and legitimize the voices and frames of the dominant classes and social groups on, for example, issues related to land, agrarian, food, and climate politics. Thus, it becomes an important task for scholar-activists to contest knowledge politics and democratize knowledge circuits, which, in turn, cannot be detached from the broader struggles for social justice.

As an academic theme and political reference point, agrarian politics in general, and the politics of land in particular, have been revitalized and restored to the global development agenda. Classic research and political questions remain and continue to be relevant, but new ones have also arisen. The range of issues is now far broader than in conventional agrarian studies. This shift partly shapes, and has been shaped, by the changing character of contemporary agrarian movements, which have undergone the ebbs and flows experienced by any social movement over time. While the era of peasant wars and agrarian movements linked to national revolutionary political projects ended some four decades ago, a significantly altered type of agrarian movement has emerged since then, and the recent transnational expressions and extensions of these have been among the most exciting developments on the global front of agrarian politics. The dimension of class and the co-constitutive axes of difference (race, ethnicity, caste, gender, generation, religion, nationality) that are dynamically at play make it challenging to understand the complexity of most contemporary agrarian movements. Their transformations into or overlap with environmental/climate justice movements as well as food movements represent some of the most important shifts in agrarian movement politics. This calls for the deployment of classic and contemporary theoretical and methodological tools of analysis in agrarian studies, combined with tools that are yet to be imagined and forged.

It is useful to see this challenge in the context of a historical and political continuum, ranging from the classic traditions established in Marx's *The Eighteenth Brumaire* and the highlights of the classic Russian agrarian populism of the second half of the nineteenth century to the core ideas about anti-capitalist struggles in the twenty-first century spelt out in Erik Olin Wright's typology of anti-capitalist struggles and Nancy Fraser's notion of 'anti-capitalist and trans-environmental struggles for eco-socialism' (Wright, 2019; Fraser, 2021).

Wright discusses five 'strategic logics' of anti-capitalist struggles, namely: 'smashing capitalism', 'dismantling capitalism', 'taming capitalism', 'resisting capitalism', and 'escaping capitalism' (2019: 38–64).

Smashing capitalism is the logic of Marxist revolutionaries; it suggests destroying a system in order to build a new one, and it requires the seizing of state power (ibid.: 42). Seizing state power occurs through 'a broad, mass-based socialist party capable of winning elections and staying in power for a sufficiently long time' (ibid.: 43). Dismantling capitalism has similar fundamental goals, although it is sceptical about a ruptural overthrow of capitalism. In its commitment to democratic socialism, the idea of this logic is to achieve a 'gradual dismantling of capitalism and the building up of the alternative through the sustained action of the state' (ibid.: 43). Smashing capitalism and dismantling capitalism both aspire to the 'ultimate possibility of replacing capitalism with a fundamentally different kind of structure, socialism' (ibid.: 44).

Taming capitalism sees capitalism as the main cause of harm in society, and advances the alternative of 'social democracy'. Its logic is anchored in the idea that 'capitalism does not need to be left to its own devices; it can be tamed by well-crafted state policies' (ibid.: 45). In other words: 'capitalism can be subjected to significant regulation and redistribution to counteract its harms and still provide adequate profits for it to function', and 'to accomplish this requires popular mobilisation and political will; one can never rely on the enlightened benevolence of elites' (ibid.: 45). Wright explains that 'the idea of taming of capitalism does not eliminate the underlying tendency for capitalism to cause harm; it simply counteracts that effect' (ibid.: 46).

Resisting capitalism advances 'struggles that oppose capitalism from outside of the state but do not themselves attempt to gain state power' (ibid.: 49), while escaping capitalism implies a degree of resignation: 'one of the oldest responses to the depredations of capitalism has been "escape"' (ibid.). The assumption here is that capitalism is too powerful to fight and defeat, and so the best that we can do is to insulate ourselves from its damaging effects, escaping 'its ravages in some sheltered environment' (ibid.).

There are two dimensions to Wright's typology: the goal of the strategy, that is, neutralizing harms or transcending structures; and the locus of strategy, namely, state or civil society. We can take three principal messages from Wright's work that are relevant to our current discussion: (i) there is a plurality and diversity of ideal-type anti-capitalist struggles; (ii) there is no single ideal-type that can be effectively deployed to fight capitalism; (iii) the key is to combine the ideal-type anti-capitalist struggles in order to erode capitalism. In short, anti-capitalist struggles are inherently pluralist, cross-class, multi-sited, and multi-scalar – just as the contemporary agrarian struggles with land struggles at their core ought to be, as discussed in Chapter 2.

For Fraser (2021), the era of climate change has made it essential that anti-capitalist struggle is co-constituted by what she calls 'trans-environmental' movements. She laments that contemporary environmental justice movements are generally concerned with the specific harm in local communities, are not sufficiently coordinated system-wide, and are not sufficiently linked to anti-capitalist struggles – meaning these 'merely environmental' movements are rarely connected to other struggles concerning, for example, social reproduction and care issues, labour conditions, and so on. She uses the term 'trans-environmental' to stress the need for an environmental movement that is able to have system-wide linkages and an anti-capitalist and eco-socialist perspective by going beyond being merely environmental. We take inspiration from Fraser's argument, and extend it to the case of agrarian movements: that is, they need to go beyond being 'merely agrarian', which is one of the key messages we have tried to convey in our discussion of the typology of land issues and struggles in Chapter 2.

Wright's and Fraser's normative concepts of struggles are a reflection of the changed global setting, including the changed agrarian world. This is a crucial backdrop for twenty-first-century agrarian scholar-activism, and differentiates it from its counterparts in the past that were heavily focused on the ideal-types of smashing/dismantling capitalism, and dominated by orthodox Marxist traditions. Today, while orthodox Marxism remains extremely influential in critical agrarian studies and agrarian advocacy work, ideological influences are more plural, diverse, and eclectic (Li, 2014; Kothari et al., 2019; Gerber, 2020; Roman-Alcalá, 2021). All this should be seen as a continuation, not a rejection, of the past: a transition from classical agrarian studies to critical agrarian studies (Borras, 2023). Within such a continuum, we should mark notable thinkers and their enduring ideas about agrarian politics and the role played by allies. The pursuit of agrarian scholar-activist work in the contemporary context calls for a 'movement-oriented' strategy. This can be understood in two senses. Firstly, it is movement-oriented because it does not shy away from linking up with and contributing to emancipatory agrarian movements and political projects. Secondly, it is movement-oriented because it aims to carry out research both individually and collectively within and through an activist research and scholar-activist movement.

The activist research and scholar-activist movement being floated here has the characteristics of a social movement: it is based upon shared broad assumptions and visions about the world as we know it and the world we want to build, as well as shared interests; it is amorphous, fluid, informal, inspired and inspiring, creative and irreverent, bold and subversive. It should take the form of a loose collective: a community of colleagues, comrades, and fellow travellers. It entails and involves formal research networks, but should not end there. It should be both orchestrated and spontaneous, able to navigate the difficult terrain between vanguardism and tailism in its relationship with agrarian movements, and should be diffuse but have clear hubs of intellectual–political imagination and creativity in an operationally polycentric manner. It should be democratically shared and dispersed across the three key sites: the academy, non-academic independent research institutions, and social movement-based research hubs. Only with such a movement can we go beyond individual agenda-setting and individual accomplishments in scholar-activist research, resolve the contradictions between the individual-centric academy and the collective-oriented social movement, and, in the process, transform scholar-activist research into a greater force for radical social change.

How can scholar-activism remain relevant and be strengthened in the contemporary context? What is to be done? Scaling up scholar-activism and transforming it into a greater force for social justice requires clarity about: (i) the aims of scholar-activist work; (ii) transformative knowledge; (iii) affirmative action; and (iv) solidarity and internationalism. The following discussion considers each of these in turn. It leans towards being normative and practical, and cuts across the three institutional settings.

Aims: Access, equity, autonomy

If the overall goal is to consolidate and expand the ranks and reach of agrarian scholar-activism, then activities and events need to have clearly spelt-out aims to make such activities effective. In this context, three overall aims of contemporary agrarian scholar-activism are crucial, and can be captured in the concepts *access*, *equity*, and *autonomy*.

The first aim is about getting basic *access* to the necessary means and conditions for effective scholar-activist work. What this entails might be different from one case to another, depending on structural and institutional histories and current circumstances, ranging from political to material. Politically, among the most basic access needs is the right to have rights (Franco et al., 2015). But we agree with Jesse Ribot's argument that 'the right to shape rights is even more important – this is the right to the means and freedoms to influence those who govern. This is emancipation' (2014: 697).

The idea and practice of scholar-activism, subversive as it is, require access to some basic civil and political rights (under domestic laws or international treaties) (Franco and Monsalve, 2018). This may sound inconsequential to scholar-activists operating in societies where liberal democratic political conditions guarantee, at least to some extent, basic freedoms to information and expression relatively free from fear of retribution. These freedoms cannot be taken for granted in some other societies marked by less-than-democratic political conditions, where participation in certain forms of advocacy could result in violent retribution from the state and elites, and the loss of jobs or even lives. Moreover, it is often in those societies in which subversive scholar-activism is most urgently needed that the most unfavourable conditions for scholar-activist work prevail. In such situations, the most urgent task for scholar-activists is to fight for the right to have rights, and the right to shape rights, to pursue a scholar-activist way of working.

There are also material and logistical requirements for effective scholar-activism, including access to research funds and research facilities such as a good library. A good library can be defined as one that is well supplied with resources, including books and subscriptions to major international scientific journals. This is crucial to researchers, enabling them to know the state of the art in different fields and disciplines at any given moment. Again, for most scholar-activists, the current distribution and extent of access to these material requirements are too limited, while only a few enjoy extensive access. This unevenness is based on the same structural and institutional conditions described above.

One of the most important material requirements in entrenching scholar-activism globally is access to language-related services and facilities. Central to this is the reality that English is the dominant language not only in the academy but also in independent research institutions and social movements. In academia today, if your academic publication is in a non-English-language journal or book, the chances are high that it will not carry the 'value' it deserves. The overwhelming majority of academic journals that are what is known as 'indexed', and are at the higher end of the journal ranking scale, are English-language journals. It is unusual to see non-English journals included among indexed journals, and even more rare to see non-English journals ranked highly in any international journal ranking system. The same applies in book publishing. Many journal and book ranking systems are based on complicated calculations that are themselves based on numbers of citations (Web of Science and Google Scholar). Because the institutional infrastructure and incentive structure are skewed in favour of English-language publications – for example, journals indexed in Web of Science are overwhelmingly in English – then Web of Science citations are also biased in favour of English-language articles. The example of institutional rewards for book publications is also telling: a book published by a Europe-based English-language publisher is likely to earn maximum incentive points for its author from the university, while a book published in Bahasa Indonesia is likely to bring minimal, if any, incentive points. But even publishing in English does not automatically level the playing field: one can receive maximum incentive points for publishing with an English-language publishing company based in the Netherlands, and few or no points for publishing with an English-language publisher in the Philippines. The structure of valuation of academic publications, within which scholar-activists are embedded, is deeply undemocratic.

Another ongoing and urgent task for scholar-activists is, therefore, to work towards dismantling such social structures – hence the need highlighted by Castree (2000) to treat universities as trenches where struggles have to be launched and sustained. Given the depth of structural and institutional bases for this undemocratic state of affairs, changing the system will be a long-term struggle. In the meantime, scholar-activists must address this challenge by fighting for access to language services. At a minimum, this means translating written and verbal communications into English, as well as language-editing support for published work. Mundane as it may sound, such support entails significant financial costs that scholar-activists – especially those situated in the Global South, and/or coming from disadvantaged social groups – may not be able to cover. Most researchers in the Global South or based in small independent research institutions or social movements do not have such resources at their disposal: indeed, such an amount may be equivalent to a full month's salary for a university researcher. Having access to resources to pay for language services and facilities is thus a basic requirement for scholar-activists, but overcoming the obstacles and constraints involved is not easy. The insights of some contemporary transnational social movements might be relevant here; they found a partial solution to a similar problem two or three decades ago through the emergence of an organized movement of 'solidarity language translators'.

The second aim relates to *equity*. The discussion above demonstrates that many potential and actual scholar-activists do not have even the minimum necessary access to some of the fundamental material and political requirements for effective scholar-activism. As discussed in earlier chapters, scholar-activist work is relational, within and outside scholar-activist circles. It is important not to see access as a stand-alone concern because doing so is likely to reinforce the problems of individualism and elitism: that is, individual access should be seen in relation to broader social structures.

It is thus important to address the question of access in the context of the inequitable structural and institutional settings within which scholar-activists – and their allies, competitors, or adversaries – are embedded.

A number of axes of inequity can be identified: among scholar-activists within and between institutional bases, characterized by social differentiation based on class and co-constitutive axes of difference; and between scholar-activists and others. As with access, inequities can be seen in the context of differentiated material and political requirements for scholar-activism. These are not random inequities, but rather a direct outcome of long histories of colonial and post-colonial systems of plunder, exploitation, and oppression, as well as contemporary power relations. It is not a random accident that a leading university in the United Kingdom is exponentially better endowed than its counterpart in Zimbabwe, for example. There are infinite manifestations of these material and political inequities.

As already suggested above, two of the most important means of knowledge production for scholar-activists are books and scientific journals, which are like a plough and land for peasants. The general pattern of distribution of access to these two key resources reflects and reproduces the axes of exploitation and oppression. If knowledge is power, then inequitable access to the means of knowledge production implies reproducing the inequitable distribution of power. The question of access is never just a technical issue, or a matter of random individual entitlement or opportunity, but an extension and reflection of the structures of power.

Ending such inequities and building a more democratic terrain on which scholar-activism can germinate, grow, and blossom are urgent imperatives. What becomes clear is that the struggle towards a more equitable distribution of the means and infrastructure for knowledge production cannot be disconnected from the broader struggles within and against capitalism.

The third aim – directly linked to the questions of access and equity discussed above – should be to produce a critical mass of multi-sited scholar-activists with a high degree of *autonomy and capacity*. This logically implies pursuing activities and events that enhance the degree of autonomy *and* capacity: that is, empowerment. To recap, by autonomy we mean the *degree* of external influence on the internal processes of a movement. This is different from the concept of 'independence', which is inherently an either/or question (Fox, 1993). Capacity relates to the ability to do what one wants to do, given necessary skills and resources. A movement may have high autonomy to do what it wants to do, but may not have the capacity to carry it out; conversely, it may have the capacity to do something but have insufficient autonomy to pursue its goals – either way, it cannot achieve its aspirations (ibid.). This is a challenge for scholar-activists regardless of institutional setting. For example, a scholar-activist may want to pursue explicitly anti-capitalist and socialist-oriented research and political advocacy, but the only available funds come from a government agency or philanthropic corporate donor. Thus, even when scholar-activists have the ability, skills, and resources to pursue their research, they may not have the necessary autonomy.

Whatever their institutional base, scholar-activists face constraints and obstacles to gaining a greater degree of autonomy and capacity. In many societies today, the prevailing political conditions tend to reduce the level of autonomy. Moreover, while many South-based universities and official research institutions are upgrading their research infrastructure and logistical investment, the levels of these generally remain far below those of their Northern counterparts. Finally, scholar-activists across all institutional spheres are socially differentiated along class and co-constitutive axes of difference (race, ethnicity, gender, generation, caste, nationality, religion, language). A privileged white person coming from an upper-class family in the North who went to a world-leading university and socialized with major global scholar-activists will not encounter the everyday constraints and obstacles to effective scholar-activism that are faced by someone who is of BIPOC (Black, Indigenous, People of

Colour) origin, low-income, attended an 'unknown' community college, and has worked in the margins of academic or activist elite circles. The degree of autonomy and the capacity of these two extreme types of scholar-activist are very different. In short, a key starting point in thinking about autonomy and capacity is a realization that the category of scholar-activism is highly differentiated along class and other axes of difference, regardless of institutional base. Failure to grasp this is likely to result in reproducing and reinforcing the social differentiation that reflects broader social structures and institutions of exploitation and oppression. Simply put, we can grasp the issue of autonomy and capacity of scholar-activists partly by understanding that the sphere of scholar-activists is not egalitarian, but is defined by hierarchy of social status and elitism.

The levels of autonomy and capacity of scholar-activists are inherently dynamic across time, and depend largely on specific projects and campaigns, institutional conditions, and funding sources. Scholar-activists are likely to be found in the continuum between the two ideal-types of high autonomy and capacity, and low autonomy and capacity. If the overall goal is to entrench scholar-activists globally across the three spheres of the academy, research institutions, and social movements, then the immediate task is to pursue activities and events that are *autonomy-building* and *capacity-enhancing* for actual and potential scholar-activists.

Transformative knowledge

Access to and equity in the means of knowledge production towards autonomy-building and capacity-enhancing activities and events are fundamental requirements for a cornerstone of scholar-activism: transformative knowledge generation, attribution, and use. Knowledge generation, attribution, and use can – and often do – reproduce structures and institutions of exploitation and oppression. One of the defining characteristics of scholar-activists, at least normatively speaking, is that they seek not just any kind of knowledge generation, attribution, and use; rather, the emphasis is on a *transformative* kind: a framework and method of work that aspire to stop knowledge infrastructure from being used to reproduce exploitation and oppression more broadly. In short, scholar-activists aspire (and ought to aspire) to an emancipatory form of knowledge generation, attribution, and use.

The current social order and hierarchy in knowledge generation reflect and reproduce the broad social system, including its characteristics of exploitation and oppression. The nature and pattern of knowledge generation are used to construct and maintain hegemonic perspectives and to justify global capitalism. Some of the basic means to produce knowledge – books, academic journals, schools, research facilities – have been generally commodified for profit. The outcome is that only a handful of countries, social groups, or individuals can afford to have full access to these means of knowledge production, leaving the vast majority in the margins. The various aspects of commodification of universities, research, and knowledge are all elements that sustain the reproduction of an unjust system. This may manifest in some mundane – seemingly harmless and even apparently positive – activities in the research world. For example, research grants, even those that are classified as scientific grants, have increasingly been aligned to support state and corporate agendas for the continuous and expanded reproduction of corporate capital. Calls for research grant applications specify pre-determined frameworks of research, such as applications for projects around market-based climate change mitigation and adaptation, or a philanthropic grant call for 'how to make the new green revolution work in Africa'. Open themes in scientific research and in policy-oriented research have become increasingly few and far between. The problems that neoliberalization has brought about in universities are global. Burawoy explains that, as public spending retreats and a university increasingly becomes a self-financing operation, 'it searches for new sources of revenue ... and cost-cutting devices' (2014: xi). He argues that:

> In competing for limited funds, universities have entered into the game of rankings, which involves elaborate and costly manipulations, subjecting scholarship to short-term calculus or arbitrary criteria that determine what counts as knowledge. The combination of commodification and rationalization has led to the polarization of conditions of higher education at every level: within and between disciplines, within and between universities, within and between countries ... Academics face a number of choices: to passively watch the process unfold, to actively participate in its promotion, or, alternatively, to uphold the university's public character and defend its autonomy by building countervailing alliances with publics that are experiencing similar pressures of marketization and rationalization (ibid.).

In the context of Burawoy's diagnosis of the current condition of universities, *knowledge attribution* is perhaps one of the most concrete manifestations of the commoditization-driven inequities in knowledge work. The neoliberalization of universities and research more generally has also meant reinforcing individual claims to intellectual property rights as individual private property, raising further dilemmas for radical scholarship and scholar-activism. As Sudbury and Okazawa-Rey correctly point out, scholar-activists are 'living with contradictions' (2009: 12), and are constantly hounded by ethical and political dilemmas. This problem is particularly acute and widespread in research related to the agrarian world, as manifested in the monetization of research participation and collaboration of individuals or organizations based in the Global South. That is, a paid collaborator who has been labelled a 'research assistant', 'data gatherer', or 'data enumerator' does not necessarily have a claim to become a co-author of the final research output. Here is a concrete hypothetical example: an academic who does not know anything about the dynamics of agrarian movements in a particular country wants to write about them, but cannot do the extensive fieldwork needed, partly because he does not know the local language. So, two seasoned local intellectual activists who know the agrarian movement in this country very well are hired as research assistants to conduct interviews and focus-group discussions on his behalf, for a fee. The fee is insignificant in the context of a well-endowed European or North American university, but is several times higher than what the local intellectuals receive as salary from a local state university or NGO. The research is carried out, data are turned over to the academic, the fee is paid to the local intellectuals, and a journal publication is released under the sole authorship of the academic who now has the individual private property rights to the data and knowledge in the article. An accompanying feature of such a lopsided system of attribution is the concept of 'private property rights' in knowledge: that is, copyright. A variant of this common practice is to casually take and use ideas from generic reports from radical non-academic organizations and movements. In this instance, usually no copyright is acknowledged because the academy considers such materials 'grey' materials, meaning something that has not strictly been 'published' in the academic definition of the term. But if these organizations want to use the copyrighted journal article that appropriated the organizations' ideas in the first place, they would be expected to reference the academic article as the 'origin' of the idea.

At first glance, we might say that there is nothing wrong, legally or even ethically, with the first hypothetical case presented here: the service buyer and the service sellers were both satisfied with the business transaction. And the activities described in both hypothetical cases are in reality quite commonly practised worldwide. However, if we use a political lens from a scholar-activist perspective, then we might assess things differently. Scholar-activists or aspiring scholar-activists should reflect on such practices more critically in *political* terms.

Similarly, there is nothing inherently wrong with the idea of a copyright, broadly speaking. But if the starting point of such a claim is a flawed system of attribution, then there is a danger of copyright formalizing a problematic attribution claim. It is equivalent to saying that there is nothing wrong with a private land title per se – as long as it is not based on a flawed system of distribution of land or problematic land claims, because then land titles can serve to formalize land-based inequality. In an extreme case, the hypothetical research assistants mentioned above could no longer reference their own knowledge about the agrarian movement without referencing the Europe-based academic who initiated the contract to do data-gathering work. Using their own knowledge without referencing the journal article of the Europe-based academic would mean that they were, legally and technically, committing plagiarism – a serious offence in the academic world. For copyright, so sacrosanct in the academy, to work fairly, it has to be based on a just system of attribution. This difficult issue brings into play a vast grey area in the academy. A few lines from Woody Guthrie's song, *This land is your land*, which was written and composed nearly a century ago in a different context and about a different issue, help illustrate the point:

> Was a high wall there that tried to stop me;
> A sign was painted said: Private Property,
> But on the backside it didn't say nothing.

We are not suggesting here that the only solution is to designate everyone who has made some contribution to a particular knowledge-generation project as co-author. What we are advocating for is a serious effort to move away from the extremely undemocratic and unfair practices captured in the somewhat caricaturized hypothetical example above, or practices close to this type. The best way forward is likely to be somewhere in between the two extremes of absolute exclusion or inclusion. If a full range of co-authorship as a way of attribution is impractical and impossible, at least being sufficiently generous in acknowledging those who make a significant contribution to the research process, which would be less logistically complicated, should be achievable. The problems with attribution described here become acute and complex because the structural and institutional architecture, and the ideological scaffolding that supports it, are so uneven and undemocratic, giving some academics and knowledge claimants within and outside the academy much greater power to make and enforce claims than others.

In this context, organic intellectuals in agrarian movements, researchers in precarious conditions, activists based in small radical independent research institutions, and agrarian movements who are kept busy fighting in the trenches could all be on the losing side of Woody's high wall. This is not to question the relevance and importance of proprietary claims to copyright, or the need for anti-plagiarism rules and enforcement. Rather, what is being floated here for further reflection is that if we have to pursue and enforce the idea of private individual copyright claims and anti-plagiarism rules, it is important to have a prior or accompanying democratization of the entire sphere of knowledge generation, attribution, circulation, and use. It cannot be that an undemocratically appropriated and claimed intellectual work can be fully protected by the legal copyright apparatus. Copyright, in principle and in practice, can only be just if it is based on a democratic system of knowledge attribution.

Of course, this is not to say that authorship should always be collaborative; there are many occasions when individual authorship is entirely appropriate and correct – including, for example, for those scholar-activists who take a break to engage with the 'force of abstraction' (Mitchell, 2004).

When we look at the balance sheet, it is those who are based in the elite circles of the academy who tend to be on the benefit side – not because they want to take advantage of 'others' through Woody's high wall, but because of the very structural and institutional setting that they are in. Some are able to exercise their agency to try to overcome the constraints and obstacles in the system, or even to radically restructure their universities in the way advocated by Castree (2000) – although that might prove to be too formidable a step for many. For example, a long-standing and long-upheld tradition in the academy with regard to collaborative co-authorship is business transactional in principle: one has to actually contribute to writing the publication. Often 'contribution' means something 'concrete', and often that something concrete means actual participation in writing the text of a manuscript. This is where the structural and institutional basis of exclusion comes into play, because making a significant enough contribution to qualify as a co-author often requires the ability to write in eloquent academic English. All too often this means that non-native English speakers, especially those from the Global South, are excluded a priori. Reducing the idea of knowledge contribution to something technical, such as the ability to write in 'academic' English, or the possession of expertise in a quantitative technique that is a key element in a publication, is perhaps the most significant de facto mechanism of exclusion, and indeed of misappropriation and misrepresentation in knowledge generation and attribution.

Meanwhile, those based in social movements, small independent research institutions, or poorly endowed universities in the Global South remain firmly on the other side of the balance sheet. In our view the best way forward for scholar-activists is process-oriented: to engage in 'bridge-building', conscious of the practical difficulties involved in trying to achieve a perfectly democratic terrain of knowledge attribution. Bridge-building may entail everyday practices such as ensuring sufficient and appropriate representation of researchers from the Global South in publication projects such as journal special issues, edited books, and so on that are directly related to the Global South. The point here is that engagement by scholar-activists in process-oriented bridge-building could make the current conditions less undemocratic.

Finally, the sphere of *knowledge use* is probably one of the most lopsided dimensions in the global knowledge complex. While the digital age has contributed to the partial erosion of the elite monopoly on information and knowledge, there are still numerous types of knowledge and information that remain inaccessible to the majority. An annual subscription to a major international journal can cost at least US$1,000, and there is no way that the many financially struggling universities, independent research institutions, and social movements (including many in the North) could afford such a cost. This leads to, among others, extreme situations where the knowledge generated by organic intellectuals in the trenches of agrarian struggles is appropriated by outsiders (allies or not, scholar-activists or not) and those same organic intellectuals cannot access the output in published format because they cannot afford to buy expensive books or subscribe to expensive journals, or – or even, and – because they cannot read English.

A positive future in terms of decolonizing and democratizing knowledge production and advancing scholar-activism requires open access for knowledge users. The struggle for this is an inherent part of struggles within and against capitalism. Production, attribution, and use are inseparable spheres of the knowledge infrastructure. Thus, another urgent task for scholar-activists is to take up the fight to decolonize and democratize access to knowledge in order to push for democratization – that is, massification – of knowledge use.

Affirmative action

Unlike pure academics operating in a neoliberalized setting based on individual competition, in which progress depends on being somehow 'better' than others, the strength of a scholar-activist rests not primarily on the achievements or importance of the individual, but on the strength of the community and collectivity. To attain and maintain such strength therefore requires constant community-building, both inside and outside the academy. This includes affirmative action. There are three social categories that ought to be the target and driving force of affirmative action: (i) those within the academy who are in or from the Global South or (ii) who are disadvantaged along the axes of social differences; and (iii) scholar-activists outside the academy.

For researchers who come from or are based in the Global South, there are social and material conditions that make it harder for them to engage in knowledge production, exchange, and use on the same terms as their counterparts from the Global North. Many of these have been enumerated above. Even when (some of) the means of knowledge production are accessible, these researchers are usually confined to working within their own country because they lack the resources and networks necessary to carry out research in other countries. Getting published, even when one has important research data and theoretical tools, can be a huge challenge due to a lack of exposure to important peer groups and networks that their Northern counterparts access easily by, for example, attending international academic conferences; having connections with key academics who are editors of, or associated with, journals; and having resources to pay for language services to reach the level of English required for publication. But even if all those hurdles can be cleared and their research is published in a top journal, it is likely to languish behind a paywall and therefore not circulate widely, while their counterparts can afford to pay for the costly option of 'Gold Open Access', ensuring permanent open access for their published work. Researchers from or based in the Global South need help to surmount all of these obstacles and overcome constraints that can be absurdly difficult.

There are also social groups who could be disadvantaged within the global academy. Such disadvantage is shaped by class and co-constitutive axes of difference: race, ethnicity, caste, gender, generation, religion, nationality. Even in some well-endowed universities in the North, researchers from these social groups face challenges in knowledge production, attribution, and use compared to their counterparts from other social groups. Thus, if you are young, female, non-Christian, a migrant BIPOC, or a non-native English-speaking researcher in Europe or North America, you are likely to face challenges that your white, male, middle- or upper-class, non-migrant counterparts do not usually face. As such, exploitative relations in the sphere of knowledge generation can be found intra-institutionally, including within a university. It is quite common to see one scholar being an 'exploiter' in one sense, while at the same time being 'exploited' in another sense.

Scholar-activists outside the academy, that is, based in social movements or small radical independent research institutions, are likely to belong to one or both of the two categories above, as well as having to confront the challenges already identified of conducting research in a non-academic setting. These researchers are likely to be on the receiving end of the most disadvantageous terms of engagement in the spheres of knowledge generation, attribution, and use.

Scholar-activists are therefore called upon to take affirmative action towards decolonizing and democratizing the structural and institutional fabric of the global spheres of knowledge production, attribution, exchange, and use by helping reduce the obstacles and remove the constraints for traditionally challenged scholar-activists. The most important way to achieve this is by helping these disadvantaged groups to form and organize social movements, which can then subversively challenge the status quo and construct a more democratic global sphere of knowledge generation, circulation, and use.

Solidarity and internationalism

Finally, scholar-activists must carry out their fundamental task of interpreting the world in various ways in order to change it, working towards greater social justice. For scholar-activists based in the academy, their site is both a refuge and a battlefield – a place of safety and a place of struggle. Responding to calls by radical geographers to connect with activists outside the academy, Castree counters:

> I want here to argue for a project of activism *within* the higher education system Leftist geographers typically feel obliged to reach out from. If this seems strange, then it is only because we have become so accustomed to thinking that activism ought to be focused 'out there', in the 'real world' (2000: 960).

We take Castree's point of treating the academy itself as a site for scholar-activism seriously (see also Burawoy, 2014; Deere, 2018).

And, as Castree goes on to point out in his essay, this can only be done collectively – as with any political struggle. Individualism and self-centrism, hallmarks of conventional academia, are polar opposites of community- and collective-oriented scholar-activism. The task requires scholar-activists to *constantly organize* and expand their ranks: a scholar-activist needs a community organizer's instinct. Alinsky's level of action – that is, local, micro, neighbourhood – may be less germane today, when bolder, bigger, multi-scalar struggles are needed, but his notion of community organizers being constantly irreverent and subversive remains just as relevant, if not more so, both inside and outside the academy.

The traditionally marginalized and resource-poor social groups in academic and scholar-activist research work are not completely powerless and resourceless. They have each other, and when they come together, they can generate a global resource pool. This can take various forms, big and small, including subverting the expensive paywall of scientific journals by maximizing the legally grey areas of online publications-sharing platforms. Actions can be taken on an individual basis and in a scattered manner; they can also be large-scale and organized, for maximum effect. Members of this marginalized social group may have something to offer to others that can be given in exchange. For example, English-language copyediting can be done, not at the open market rates determined in the Global North, but at affordable 'solidarity rates', or even on the basis of in-kind exchanges. Contemporary transnational social justice movements would not have emerged without an organized activist corps of language interpreters and translators. It is hard to imagine how the struggle to democratize the global terrain of knowledge production, circulation, and use can be achieved without the participation of an organized activist corps of translators and editors. How this can be organized, at scale, still needs to be determined.

Global networking is key in knowledge production, circulation, and use. Simply put, it is about one's insertion into the web of power: in the current context, this means an academic's insertion into and location in the web of political power within the academy, and the web of power between the academy and settings outside the academy (Derickson and Routledge, 2015: 5). Location in power webs manifests in various ways and forms. Particularly in the academy, it is organized by discipline, field, and theme, or by country and world region. These networks are crucial in terms of taking the pulse of the field, knowing the state of the art, following the latest debates, being aware of key researchers in one's field, receiving peer feedback on ideas and draft documents, forging alliances for stronger research teams that could win competitive grants or collaboratively write high-impact publications, and so on. It is also through such networks that one gets to know editors of book series for elite university presses, or editors of prestigious journals. Many of the conventional academic networks and associations require membership fees, and organize regular international conferences. Many (not all) are akin to elite membership-based clubs.

Many researchers in the traditionally marginalized social groups, including scholar-activists, struggle to get themselves inserted into these networks and elite circles for various reasons, but often because of the prohibitive costs of regular international travel, difficulty in getting visas, membership fees, their inability to engage on the basis of the state of the art, the prevailing English-language requirements, and so on. Instead of passively accepting exclusion from elite networks, scholar-activists from the traditionally marginalized groups can build their own parallel, complementary, and/or alternative network. This will not immediately eliminate the structural and institutional constraints and obstacles they face, but it could signify the beginning of a more organized effort to do so. It would be interesting to see two parallel networks that could become either competitive or complementary: one that is akin to an elitist membership-only club that is comfortable with the status quo in the academy; the other more closely resembling a multi-sited version of Alinsky's irreverent neighbourhood associations, aimed at subverting the status quo in the global academy.

The task of dismantling the structural and institutional basis for the undemocratic world of knowledge generation, attribution, and use is daunting and extremely difficult. It cannot be divorced from the broader struggles within and against capitalism. While networks among scholar-activists are necessary, it is important that such efforts are transformed into a coherent emancipatory movement of scholar-activists based on *solidarity and internationalism*. This means not only emphasizing the need to address the everyday practical concerns of individual scholar-activists or agrarian movement organizations in specific places and times, but also linking the struggle for a democratic sphere of knowledge generation, exchange, and use to the broader struggles within and against capitalism. A solidarity-based scholar-activist movement is a counter-current to the individualistic, opportunistic, narcissistic norm in the academy, puts a premium on the broad moral economy principle of progressing or starving together, and makes sure no one is left behind. Internationalism is key to countering the economic debt perpetuated by northern and western countries. Broadly inspired by concepts such as 'ecological debt' and 'climate debt', we use 'academic debt' here to mean the debt that is owed by former colonizing and imperialist nations, whose plunder of many countries in the Global South resulted in long-term destruction of the autonomy and capacity of those countries to build their own robust academic institutions that are not subservient, materially and ideologically, to their counterparts in the global imperial centres. Internationalism means forging coalitions among scholar-activists globally in order to tackle this academic debt and construct a global scholar-activism that is truly emancipatory.

*****

For us, land struggles that are not linked to broader struggles against capitalism can be dramatic but will not significantly change the world as we know it. Struggles within and against capitalism without any appropriate understanding of and connection to agrarian struggles are bound to fail. The more promising struggles are going beyond merely agrarian:

that is, they are linking various class and sectoral struggles within the rural and agrarian world to form anti-systemic struggles, and are in turn connected to anti-capitalist struggles across the board (Wright, 2019; Fraser, 2021). The task of building such a global anti-capitalist movement in which land struggles are a core part requires the contribution of public intellectuals, in the sense that Gramsci (1971) intended. And for this task, all types of knowledge politics will be necessary: progressive, radical, activist, and scholar-activist.

Ultimately, scholar-activists – even those who come from the socially marginalized groups – by definition belong to a better-off subcategory in the broader social hierarchy of those at the receiving end of exploitation and oppression. It is tempting to do scholar-activist work *for* the exploited and oppressed, and there is a material basis for doing so. It represents a revolutionary and emancipatory knowledge and a form of radical political advocacy work. This type of radical scholarship may be the most important of all progressive and revolutionary types of knowledge production, and could be far more expansive. But for us, it is not what decisively defines a scholar-activist. Writing *for and with* the exploited and oppressed is a small subcategory of this radical scholarship, but it is an important subcategory. This implies that scholar-activists are those who commit themselves to disorderly political movements, as argued above on the basis of Frances Fox Piven's work. Despite the constant tensions that exist between scholar-activists, as narrowly defined in this book, on the one side and other knowledge producers, brokers, and users, radical or otherwise, on the other, they are not necessarily or automatically adversaries. On many occasions and for many issues, they could be allies for the common good.

In conclusion: worldwide, land struggles are most likely going to intensify and expand in the near future in light of the growing mainstream consensus around so-called nature-based solutions to climate change such as reaching net zero emissions via carbon offset projects that are likely to result in more land grabs. This will render agrarian scholar-activism even more urgent and necessary. There is no getting around the fact that scholar-activists have a dual task: to excel in academic work and in political work. This takes an enormous commitment of time and effort. In this context, agrarian scholar-activists, wherever they are located, sometimes feel that they are like the Chayanovian peasants: their production is not fully commercially oriented or viable, much of their labour is non-remunerated, their contribution to broader society is largely unrecognized, and their operation does not bring much profit and always tends to just break even. In order to survive, they have to resort to self-exploitation, combining long working hours with self-denial that may even extend to some necessities in life. Yet they feel a profound sense of fulfilment that cannot be measured in purely material or monetary ways. We will give the last words to Piven, who captures fully and powerfully a sentiment that we believe most agrarian scholar-activists would agree with.

> Scholar-activists should stop regarding themselves as martyrs. We are activists because of the joy political work gives us, because even when we fail, working to make our society kinder, fairer, more just, gives a satisfaction like no other, because the comrades we find in the effort are friends like no other, and also because our activist efforts illuminate our social and political world in ways that scholarship alone never can (2010: 810).

References

Adnan, S. (2013) 'Land grabs and primitive accumulation in deltaic Bangladesh: Interactions between neoliberal globalization, state interventions, power relations and peasant resistance', *Journal of Peasant Studies* 40(1): 87–128.

Agarwal, B. (1994) *A Field of One's Own: Gender and Land Rights in South Asia*, Cambridge University Press, Cambridge.

Agarwal, B. (2014) 'Food sovereignty, food security and democratic choice: Critical contradictions, difficult conciliations', *Journal of Peasant Studies* 41(6): 1247–1268.

Ajl, M. (2021) *A People's Green New Deal*, Pluto Press, London.

Akram-Lodhi, A.H. (2021) 'The ties that bind? Agroecology and the agrarian question in the twenty-first century', *Journal of Peasant Studies* 48(4): 687–714.

Akram-Lodhi, A.H. and Kay, C. (2010a) 'Surveying the agrarian question (part 1): Unearthing foundations, exploring diversity', *Journal of Peasant Studies* 37(1): 177–202.

Akram-Lodhi, A.H. and Kay, C. (2010b) 'Surveying the agrarian question (part 2): Current debates and beyond', *Journal of Peasant Studies* 37(2): 255–284.

Akram-Lodhi, A.H., Borras Jr, S.M. and Kay, C. (2007) *Land, Poverty and Livelihoods in an Era of Globalization: Perspectives from Developing and Transition Countries*, Routledge, London.

Alinsky, S. (1969 [orig. 1946]) *Reveille for Radicals*, Vintage, New York.

Alinsky, S. (1971) *Rules for Radicals: A Pragmatic Primer for Realistic Radicals*, Vintage, New York.

Alonso-Fradejas, A. (2021) '"Leaving no one unscathed" in sustainability transitions: The life purging agro-extractivism of corporate renewables', *Journal of Rural Studies* 81: 127–138.

Altieri, M.A. and Toledo, V.M. (2011) 'The agroecological revolution in Latin America: Rescuing nature, ensuring food sovereignty and empowering peasants', *Journal of Peasant Studies* 38(3): 587–612.

Andrade, D. (2020) 'Populism from above and below: The path to regression in Brazil', *Journal of Peasant Studies* 47(7): 1470–1496.

Andreas, J., Kale, S.S., Levien, M. and Zhang, Q.F. (2020) 'Rural land dispossession in China and India', *Journal of Peasant Studies* 47(6): 1109–1142.

Arboleda, M. (2020) 'Towards an agrarian question of circulation: Walmart's expansion in Chile and the agrarian political economy of supply chain capitalism', *Journal of Agrarian Change* 20(3): 345–363.

Arsel, M. and Büscher, B. (2012) 'Nature™ Inc.: Changes and continuities in neoliberal conservation and market-based environmental policy', *Development and Change* 43(1): 53–78.

Arsel, M., Hogenboom, B. and Pellegrini, L. (2016) 'The extractive imperative in Latin America', *The Extractive Industries and Society* 3(4): 880–887.

Ashwood, L., Canfield, J., Fairbairn, M. and De Master, K. (2020) 'What owns the land: The corporate organization of farmland investment', *Journal of Peasant Studies* 49(2): 233–262.

Bachriadi, D. (2010) *Between Discourse and Action: Agrarian Reform and Rural Social Movements in Indonesia Post-1965*, PhD dissertation, Adelaide, South Australia: University of Flinders.

Baksh-Soodeen, R. and Harcourt, W. (eds) (2015) *The Oxford Handbook of Transnational Feminist Movements*, Oxford University Press, New York.

Barbesgaard, M. (2018) 'Blue growth: Savior or ocean grabbing?', *Journal of Peasant Studies* 45(1): 130–149.

Baud, M. and Rutten, R. (2004) *Popular Intellectuals and Social Movements: Framing Protest in Asia, Africa, and Latin America*, Cambridge University Press, Cambridge.

Baviskar, A. and Levien, M. (2021) 'Farmers' protests in India: Introduction to the JPS Forum', *Journal of Peasant Studies* 48(7): 1341–1355.

Bello, W. (2003) *Deglobalization: Ideas for a New World Economy*, Zed, London.

Benjaminsen, T.A. and Bryceson, I. (2012) 'Conservation, green/blue grabbing and accumulation by dispossession in Tanzania', *Journal of Peasant Studies* 39(2): 335–355.

Bernstein, H. (2006) 'Is there an agrarian question in the twenty-first century?', *Canadian Journal of Development Studies/Revue canadienne d'études du développement* 27(4): 449–460.

Bernstein, H. (2010) *Class Dynamics of Agrarian Change*. Fernwood, Halifax (NS); Practical Action Publishing, Rugby.
Bernstein, H. (2014) 'Food sovereignty via the "peasant way": A sceptical view', *Journal of Peasant Studies* 41(6): 1031–1063.
Bernstein, H. (2018) 'The "peasant problem" in the Russian revolution(s), 1905–1929', *Journal of Peasant Studies* 45(5–6): 1127–1150.
Bernstein, H. and Byres, T. (2001) 'From peasant studies to agrarian change', *Journal of Agrarian Change* 1(1): 1–56.
Bhattacharya, T. (2017) *Social reproduction theory: Remapping class, recentering oppression*, Pluto, London.
Biekart, K. and Jelsma, M. (eds) (1994) *Peasants Beyond Protest in Central America*, Transnational Institute (TNI), Amsterdam.
Borras Jr, S.M. (2020) 'Agrarian social movements: The absurdly difficult but not impossible agenda of defeating right-wing populism and exploring a socialist future', *Journal of Agrarian Change*, 20(1): 3–36.
Borras, Jr. S.M. (2023) 'Politically engaged, pluralist and internationalist: Critical agrarian studies today', *Journal of Peasant Studies* <https://doi.org/10.1080/03066150.2022.2163164>.
Borras Jr, S.M. and Franco, J.C. (2009) 'Transnational agrarian movements struggling for land and citizenship rights'. IDS Working Papers, 2009(323), 01–44, Institute of Development Studies, Brighton.
Borras Jr, S.M. and Franco, J.C. (2013) 'Global land grabbing and political reactions "from below"', *Third World Quarterly* 34(9): 1723–1747.
Borras Jr, S.M. and Franco, J.C. (2018) 'The challenge of locating land-based climate change mitigation and adaptation politics within a social justice perspective: Towards an idea of agrarian climate justice', *Third World Quarterly* 39(7): 1308–1325.
Borras Jr, S.M., Franco, J.C., Gómez, S., Kay, C. and Spoor, M. (2012) 'Land grabbing in Latin America and the Caribbean', *Journal of Peasant Studies* 39(3–4): 845–872.
Borras Jr, S.M., Franco, J.C., Isakson, R., Levidow, L. and Vervest, P. (2016) 'The rise of flex crops and commodities: Implications for research', *Journal of Peasant Studies* 43(1): 93–115.
Borras Jr, S.M., Franco, J.C. and Nam, Z. (2020) 'Climate change and land: Insights from Myanmar', *World Development* 129: 104864.

Borras Jr, S.M., Franco, J.C., Ra, D., Kramer, T., Kamoon, M., Phyu, P., ... and Ye, J. (2021) 'Rurally rooted cross-border migrant workers from Myanmar, Covid-19, and agrarian movements', *Agriculture and Human Values* 39: 315–338.

Borras Jr, S.M., Scoones, I., Baviskar, A., Edelman, M., Peluso, N.L. and Wolford, W. (2022a) 'Climate change and agrarian struggles: An invitation to contribute to a JPS Forum', *Journal of Peasant Studies* 49(1): 1–28.

Borras Jr, S.M., Franco, J.C., Moreda, T., Xu, Y., Bruna, N. and Demena, B. A. (2022b) 'The value of so-called 'failed' large-scale land acquisitions', *Land Use Policy* 119: 106199.

Brem-Wilson, J. (2014) 'From "here" to "there": Social movements, the academy and solidarity research', *Socialist Studies/Études Socialistes* 10(1): 111–132.

Brenner, N. and Schmid, C. (2014) 'The 'urban age' in question', *International Journal of Urban and Regional Research* 38(3): 731–755.

Brent, Z.W. (2015) 'Territorial restructuring and resistance in Argentina', *Journal of Peasant Studies* 42(3–4): 671–694.

Brockington, D. (2002) *Fortress Conservation: The Preservation of the Mkomazi Game Reserve*, Tanzania, Indiana University Press.

Brockington, D. and Duffy, R. (eds) (2011) *Capitalism and Conservation*, John Wiley & Sons, London.

Burawoy, M. (2014) 'Foreword', in A. Hanemaayer and C. Schneider (eds), *The Public Sociology Debate: Ethics and Engagement*, pp. ix–xviii, University of British Columbia Press, Vancouver (BC).

Burchardt, H.J. and Dietz, K. (2014) '(Neo-) extractivism: A new challenge for development theory from Latin America', *Third World Quarterly* 35(3): 468–486.

Burnett, K. and Murphy, S. (2014) 'What place for international trade in food sovereignty?', *Journal of Peasant Studies* 41(6): 1065–1084.

Büscher, B., Sullivan, S., Neves, K., Igoe, J. and Brockington, D. (2012) 'Towards a synthesized critique of neoliberal biodiversity conservation', *Capitalism Nature Socialism* 23(2): 4–30.

Byres, T.J. (1979) 'Of neo-populist pipe-dreams: Daedalus in the Third World and the myth of urban bias', *Journal of Peasant Studies* 6(2): 210–244.

Byres, T.J. (1981) 'The new technology, class formation and class action in the Indian countryside', *Journal of Peasant Studies* 8(4): 405–454.
Byres, T.J. (2004) 'Neo-classical neo-populism 25 years on: Déjà vu and déjà passé. Towards a critique', *Journal of Agrarian Change* 4(1–2): 17–44.
Calmon, D., Jacovetti, C. and Koné, M. (2021) 'Agrarian climate justice as a progressive alternative to climate security: Mali at the intersection of natural resource conflicts', *Third World Quarterly* 42(12): 2785–2803.
Caouette, D. and Turner, S. (eds) (2009) *Agrarian Angst and Rural Resistance in Contemporary Southeast Asia*, Routledge, London.
Carolan, M. (2020) 'Automated agrifood futures: Robotics, labor and the distributive politics of digital agriculture', *Journal of Peasant Studies* 47(1): 184–207.
Carter, M. (ed.) (2015) *Challenging Social Inequality: The Landless Rural Workers' Movement and Agrarian Reform in Brazil*, Duke University Press, Durham (NC).
Castree, N. (2000) 'Professionalisation, activism, and the university: Whither "critical geography"?', *Environment and Planning A: Economy and Space* 32(6): 955–970.
Chagnon, C.W., Durante, F., Gills, B.K., Hagolani-Albov, S.E., Hokkanen, S., Kangasluoma, S.M., ... and Vuola, M.P. (2022) 'From extractivism to global extractivism: the evolution of an organizing concept', *Journal of Peasant Studies* 49(4): 760–792.
Chambati, W. (2017) 'Changing forms of wage labour in Zimbabwe's new agrarian structure', *Agrarian South: Journal of Political Economy* 6(1): 79–112.
Chayanov, A.V. (1966 [orig. 1925]) *The Theory of the Peasant Economy*, Manchester University Press, Manchester.
Choudry, A. (2020) 'Reflections on academia, activism, and the politics of knowledge and learning', *The International Journal of Human Rights* 24(1): 28–45.
Claeys, P. (2015) *Human Rights and the Food Sovereignty Movement: Reclaiming Control*, Routledge, London.
Claeys, P. and Delgado Pugley, D. (2017) 'Peasant and indigenous transnational social movements engaging with climate justice', *Canadian Journal of Development Studies/Revue canadienne d'études du développement* 38(3): 325–340.

Claeys, P. and Edelman, M. (2020) 'The United Nations Declaration on the rights of peasants and other people working in rural areas', *Journal of Peasant Studies* 47(1): 1–68.

Clapp, J. (2014) 'Financialization, distance and global food politics', *Journal of Peasant Studies* 41(5): 797–814.

Clapp, J., Newell, P. and Brent, Z.W. (2018) 'The global political economy of climate change, agriculture and food systems', *Journal of Peasant Studies* 45(1): 80–88.

Corbera, E. (2012) 'Problematizing REDD+ as an experiment in payments for ecosystem services', *Current Opinion in Environmental Sustainability* 4(6): 612–619.

Coronado, S. (2019) 'Rights in the time of populism: land and institutional change amid the re-emergence of right-wing authoritarianism in Colombia', *Land*, 8(8): 119.

Coronado, S. (2022) *Peasants, Protests and Litigation: Struggles over land and institutions in Colombia*, PhD dissertation, The Hague: International Institute of Social Studies.

Corrado, A., de Castro, C. and Perrotta, D. (eds) (2016) *Migration and Agriculture: Mobility and Change in the Mediterranean Area*, Routledge, London.

Cotula, L. (2013) 'The international political economy of the global land rush: A critical appraisal of trends, scale, geography and drivers', in B. White et al. (eds) *The New Enclosures: Critical Perspectives on Corporate Land Deals*, pp. 43–74, Routledge, London.

Cousins, B. (2022) 'Land, social reproduction and agrarian change', in S.M. Borras Jr and J.C. Franco (eds), *The Oxford Handbook of Land*. Oxford University Press, Oxford.

Croteau, D. (2005) 'Which side are you on? The tension between movement scholarship and activism', in D. Croteau et al. (eds), *Rhyming Hope and History: Activists, Academics, and Social Movement Scholarship*, pp. 20–40, University of Minnesota Press, Minneapolis (MN).

Croteau, D., Haynes, W. and Ryan, C. (2005) 'Integrating social movement theory and practice', in D. Croteau et al. (eds), *Rhyming Hope and History: Activists, Academics, and Social Movement Scholarship*', pp. xi–xviii, University of Minnesota Press, Minneapolis (MN).

Daigle, M. (2019) 'Tracing the terrain of Indigenous food sovereignties', *Journal of Peasant Studies* 46(2): 297–315.

Davis, J., Moulton, A.A., Van Sant, L. and Williams, B. (2019) 'Anthropocene, capitalocene, plantationocene? A manifesto for ecological justice in an age of global crises', *Geography Compass* 13(5): e12438.

Day, A.F. and Schneider, M. (2018) 'The end of alternatives? Capitalist transformation, rural activism and the politics of possibility in China', *Journal of Peasant Studies* 45(7): 1221–1246.

Deere, C.D. (1995) 'What difference does gender make? Rethinking peasant studies', *Feminist Economics* 1(1): 53–72.

Deere, C.D. (2018) 'The practice of Latin American studies: dilemmas of scholarly communication', *Lasa Forum* 49(3): 7–23.

Deininger, K. (2011) 'Challenges posed by the new wave of farmland investment', *Journal of Peasant Studies* 38(2): 217–247.

Deininger, K. and Binswanger, H. (1999) 'The evolution of the World Bank's land policy: Principles, experience, and future challenges', *The World Bank Research Observer* 14(2): 247–276.

De Janvry, A., Gordillo, G., Platteau, J-P. and Sadoulet, E. (eds) (2001) *Access to Land, Rural Poverty, and Public Action*, Oxford University Press, Oxford.

de Jong, S., Icaza, R., Vázquez, R. and Withaeckx, S. (2017) 'Editorial: Decolonising the University', *Tijdschrift voor Genderstudies* 20(3): 227–231.

Delgado-Wise, R. and Veltmeyer, H. (2016) *Agrarian Change, Migration and Development*, Fernwood, Halifax (NS); Practical Action Publishing, Rugby.

Dell'Angelo, J., D'Odorico, P., Rulli, M.C. and Marchand, P. (2017) 'The tragedy of the grabbed commons: Coercion and dispossession in the global land rush', *World Development* 92: 1–12.

Derickson, K. and Routledge, P. (2015) 'Resourcing scholar-activism: Collaboration, transformation, and the production of knowledge', *The Professional Geographer* 67(1): 1–7.

de Schutter, O. (2011) 'How not to think of land grabbing: Three critiques of large-scale investments in farmland', *Journal of Peasant Studies* 38(2): 249–279.

Deslippe, D., Fure-Slocum, E. and McKerley, J.W. (2016) 'Introduction: Challenges of engaged scholarship and teaching', in D. Deslippe, E. Fure-Slocum and J.W. McKerley (eds),

Civic Labors: Scholar Activism and Working-class Studies, pp. 1–10, University of Illinois Press, Champaign (IL).

Desmarais, A. (2007) *La Via Campesina: Globalization and the Power of Peasants*, Fernwood, Halifax (NS); Pluto, London.

de Wit, M.M., Shattuck, A., Iles, A., Graddy-Lovelace, G., Roman-Alcalá, A. and Chappell, M.J. (2021) 'Operating principles for collective scholar-activism', *Journal of Agriculture, Food Systems, and Community Development* 10(2): 1–19.

Diskin, M. (1989) 'El Salvador: Reform prevents change', in W. Thiesenhusen (ed.), *Searching for Agrarian Reform in Latin America*, pp. 429–450. Unwin Hyman.

Dressler, W.H. and Guieb III, E.R. (2015) 'Violent enclosures, violated livelihoods: Environmental and military territoriality in a Philippine frontier', *Journal of Peasant Studies* 42(2): 323–345.

Duncan, J., Claeys, P., Rivera-Ferre, M.G., Oteros-Rozas, E., Van Dyck, B., Plank, C. and Desmarais, A.A. (2021) 'Scholar-activists in an expanding European food sovereignty movement', *Journal of Peasant Studies* 48(4): 875–900.

Dunlap, A. (2018) 'Counterinsurgency for wind energy: The Bíi Hioxo wind park in Juchitán, Mexico', *Journal of Peasant Studies* 45(3): 630–652.

Dwyer, M.B. (2015) 'The formalization fix? Land titling, land concessions and the politics of spatial transparency in Cambodia', *Journal of Peasant Studies* 42(5): 903–928.

Edelman, M. (1999) *Peasants Against Globalization: Rural Social Movements in Costa Rica*, Stanford University Press, Stanford (CA).

Edelman, M. (2009) 'Synergies and tensions between rural social movements and professional researchers', *Journal of Peasant Studies* 36(1): 245–265.

Edelman, M. (2013) 'What is a peasant? What are peasantries? A briefing paper on issues of definition', First session of the Intergovernmental Working Group on a United Nations Declaration on the Rights of Peasants and Other People Working in Rural Areas, Geneva, July, 15–19.

Edelman, M. (2021) 'Hollowed out Heartland, USA: How capital sacrificed communities and paved the way for authoritarian populism', *Journal of Rural Studies* 82: 505–517.

Edelman, M. and Borras Jr, S.M. (2016) *Political Dynamics of Transnational Agrarian Movements*, Fernwood, Halifax (NS); Practical Action Publishing, Rugby.

Edelman, M. and León, A. (2013) 'Cycles of land grabbing in Central America: An argument for history and a case study in the Bajo Aguán, Honduras', *Third World Quarterly* 34(9): 1697–1722.

Edelman, M. and Wolford, W. (2017) 'Introduction: Critical agrarian studies in theory and practice', *Antipode* 49(4): 959–976.

Edelman, M., Oya, C. and Borras Jr, S.M. (2013) 'Global land grabs: Historical processes, theoretical and methodological implications and current trajectories', *Third World Quarterly* 34(9): 1517–1531.

Engels, F. (1894) *The peasant question in France and Germany* <https://www.marxists.org/archive/marx/works/1894/peasant-question/index.htm> [downloaded 11 February 2019].

Fairbairn, M. (2014) '"Like gold with yield": Evolving intersections between farmland and finance', *Journal of Peasant Studies* 41(5): 777–795.

Fairbairn, M. (2020) *Fields of Gold: Financing the Global Land Rush*, Cornell University Press, Ithaca (NY).

Fairhead, J., Leach, M. and Scoones, I. (2012) 'Green grabbing: A new appropriation of nature?', *Journal of Peasant Studies* 39(2): 237–261.

Fameree, C. (2016) 'Political contestations around land deals: Insights from Peru', *Canadian Journal of Development Studies/Revue canadienne d'études du développement* 37(4): 541–559.

Fernandes, B.M. (2013) 'Re-peasantization, resistance and subordination: The struggle for land and agrarian reform in Brazil', *Agrarian South: Journal of Political Economy* 2(3): 269–289.

Foster, J.B. (1999) 'Marx's theory of metabolic rift: Classical foundations for environmental sociology', *American Journal of Sociology* 105(2): 366–405.

Fox, J. (1990) 'Editor's introduction', in J. Fox (ed.), *The Challenge of Rural Democratisation: Perspectives from Latin America and the Philippines*, pp. 1–14, Frank Cass, London.

Fox, J. (1993) 'State–society interaction and distributive reform in Mexico', in J. Fox (ed.), *The Politics of Food in Mexico: State Power and Social Mobilization, Food Systems and Agrarian Change*, pp. 12–44, Cornell University Press, Ithaca (NY).

Fox, J. (2006) 'Lessons from action-research partnerships: LASA/Oxfam America 2004 Martin Diskin Memorial Lecture', *Development in Practice* 16(1): 27–38.

Fox, J. (2010) 'Coalitions and networks', in H. Anheier and S. Toepler (eds), *International Encyclopedia of Civil Society*, pp. 41–82, Springer, New York.

Franco, J.C. (2001) *Elections and Democratization in Philippines*, Routledge, London.

Franco, J.C. (2008a) 'Making land rights accessible: Social movements and political-legal innovation in the rural Philippines', *Journal of Development Studies* 44(7): 991–1022.

Franco, J.C. (2008b) 'Peripheral justice? Rethinking justice sector reform in the Philippines', *World Development* 36(10): 1858–1873.

Franco, J.C. (2014) 'Reclaiming Free Prior and Informed Consent (FPIC) in the context of global land grabs', Transnational Institute (TNI), Amsterdam.

Franco, J.C. and Borras Jr, S.M. (eds) (2013) *Land Concentration, Land Grabbing and People's Struggles in Europe*, European Coordination Via Campesina (ECVC), Mons; Hands off the Land Network, Transnational Institute (TNI), Amsterdam.

Franco, J.C. and Borras Jr, S.M. (2019) 'Grey areas in green grabbing: Subtle and indirect interconnections between climate change politics and land grabs and their implications for research', *Land Use Policy* 84: 192–199.

Franco, J.C. and Borras Jr, S.M. (2021) 'The global climate of land politics', *Globalizations* 18(7): 1277–1297.

Franco, J.C. and Monsalve Suárez, S. (2018) 'Why wait for the state? Using the CFS Tenure Guidelines to recalibrate political-legal struggles for democratic land control', *Third World Quarterly*, 39(7), 1386–1402.

Franco, J.C., Levidow, L., Fig, D., Goldfarb, L., Hönicke, M. and Luisa Mendonça, M. (2010) 'Assumptions in the European Union biofuels policy: Frictions with experiences in Germany, Brazil and Mozambique', *Journal of Peasant Studies* 37(4): 661–698.

Franco, J.C., Mehta, L. and Veldwisch, G.J. (2013) 'The global politics of water grabbing', *Third World Quarterly* 34(9): 1651–1675.

Franco, J.C., Monsalve, S. and Borras Jr, S.M. (2015) 'Democratic land control and human rights', *Current Opinion in Environmental Sustainability* 15: 66–71.

Fraser, A. (2019) 'Land grab/data grab: Precision agriculture and its new horizons', *Journal of Peasant Studies* 46(5): 893–912.

Fraser, N. (2021) 'Climates of capital: For a trans-environmental eco-socialism', *New Left Review* 127: 94–127.
Friedmann, H. and McMichael, P. (1989) 'The rise and decline of national agricultures, 1870 to the present', *Sociologia ruralis* 29(2): 93–117.
Gaventa, J. and Tandon, R. (2010) *Globalising Citizens: New Dynamics of Inclusion and Exclusion*, Zed, London.
Gerber, J.F. (2020) 'Degrowth and critical agrarian studies', *Journal of Peasant Studies* 47(2): 235–264.
Gilbert, J. (2015) *Planning Democracy: Agrarian Intellectuals and the Intended New Deal*, Yale University Press, New Haven (CT).
GRAIN (2008) *Seized*, Barcelona, GRAIN
GRAIN (2013) 'Collating and dispersing: GRAIN's strategies and methods', *Journal of Peasant Studies* 40(3): 531–536.
Grajales, J. (2011) 'The rifle and the title: Paramilitary violence, land grab and land control in Colombia', *Journal of Peasant Studies* 38(4): 771–792.
Gramsci, A. (1971) *Selections from the Prison Notebooks*, International Publishers, New York.
Greenwood, D. (2006) 'Theoretical research, applied research, and action research', in C. Hale (ed.), *Engaging Contradictions: Theory, Politics, and Methods of Activist Scholarship*, pp. 319–340, University of California Press, Berkeley (CA).
Griffin, K., Khan, A.R. and Ickowitz, A. (2002) 'Poverty and distribution of land', *Journal of Agrarian Change* 2(3): 279–330.
Gyapong, A.Y. (2019) 'Land deals, wage labour, and everyday politics', *Land* 8(6): 94.
Hale, C. (2006) 'Activist research v. cultural critique: Indigenous land rights and the contradictions of politically engaged anthropology', *Cultural Anthropology* 21(1): 96–120.
Hale, C. (2008) 'Introduction', in C. Hale (ed.), *Engaging Contradictions: Theory, Politics, and Methods of Activist Scholarship*, pp. 1–30, University of California Press, Berkeley (CA).
Hall, D., Hirsch, P. and Li, T. (2010) *Powers of Exclusion: Land Dilemmas in Southeast Asia*, NUS University Press, Singapore.
Hall, R. (2011) 'Land grabbing in Southern Africa: The many faces of the investor rush', *Review of African Political Economy* 38(128): 193–214.

Hall, R., Edelman, M., Borras Jr, S.M., Scoones, I., White, B. and Wolford, W. (2015) 'Resistance, acquiescence or incorporation? An introduction to land grabbing and political reactions "from below"', *Journal of Peasant Studies* 42(3–4): 467–488.

Hall, R., Scoones, I. and Tsikata, D. (2017) 'Plantations, outgrowers and commercial farming in Africa: Agricultural commercialisation and implications for agrarian change', *Journal of Peasant Studies* 44(3): 515–537.\

Harriss-White, B. (2022) 'Petty commodity production'. *Journal of Peasant Studies*, 1–20 <https://doi.org/10.1080/03066150.2022.2138354>.

Harvey, N. (1998) *The Chiapas Rebellion: The Struggle for Land and Democracy*, Duke University Press, Durham (NC).

Henderson, T.P. (2018) 'The class dynamics of food sovereignty in Mexico and Ecuador', *Journal of Agrarian Change* 18(1): 3–21.

Hisano, S., Akitsu, M. and McGreevy, S.R. (2018) 'Revitalising rurality under the neoliberal transformation of agriculture: Experiences of re-agrarianisation in Japan', *Journal of Rural Studies* 61: 290–301.

Ho, P. (2001) 'Who owns China's land? Policies, property rights and deliberate institutional ambiguity', *The China Quarterly* 166: 394–421.

Hobsbawm, E. (1973) 'Peasants and politics', *Journal of Peasant Studies* 1(1): 3–22.

Holleman, H. (2018) *Dust Bowls of Empire*, Yale University Press, New Haven (CT).

Holt-Giménez, E. and Shattuck, A. (2011) 'Food crises, food regimes and food movements: Rumblings of reform or tides of transformation?', *Journal of Peasant Studies* 38(1): 109–144.

Holt-Giménez, E., Shattuck, A. and Van Lammeren, I. (2021) 'Thresholds of resistance: Agroecology, resilience and the agrarian question', *Journal of Peasant Studies* 48(4): 715–733.

Hospes, O. (2014) 'Food sovereignty: The debate, the deadlock, and a suggested detour', *Agriculture and Human Values* 31(1): 119–130.

Huizer, G. (1975) 'How peasants become revolutionaries: Some cases from Latin America and Southeast Asia', *Development and Change* 6(3): 27–56.

Hunsberger, C., Corbera, E., Borras Jr, S.M., Franco, J.C., Woods, K., Work, C., ... and Vaddhanaphuti, C. (2017) 'Climate change mitigation, land grabbing and conflict: Towards a landscape-based and collaborative action research agenda', *Canadian Journal of Development Studies* 38(3): 305–324.

Iles, A. (2022) 'Sustaining agrarian struggles through painting invasion and resistance: the work of BoyD', *Journal of Peasant Studies* 49(6): 1348–1354.

Isakson, S.R. (2014) 'Food and finance: The financial transformation of agro-food supply chains', *Journal of Peasant Studies* 41(5): 749–775.

Ito, T., Rachman, N.F. and Savitri, L.A. (2014) 'Power to make land dispossession acceptable: A policy discourse analysis of the Merauke Integrated Food and Energy Estate (MIFEE), Papua, Indonesia', *Journal of Peasant Studies* 41(1): 29–50.

Jacobs, R. (2018) 'An urban proletariat with peasant characteristics: Land occupations and livestock raising in South Africa', *Journal of Peasant Studies* 45(5–6): 884–903.

Jansen, K. (2015) 'The debate on food sovereignty theory: Agrarian capitalism, dispossession and agroecology', *Journal of Peasant Studies* 42(1): 213–232.

Jodhka, S.S. (2021) 'Why are the farmers of Punjab protesting?' *Journal of Peasant Studies*, 48(7), 1356–1370.

Kautsky, K. (1988 [orig. 1899]) *The Agrarian Question* (Vol. 1), Zwan, London.

Kay, C. (2002) 'Why East Asia overtook Latin America: Agrarian reform, industrialization and development', *Third World Quarterly* 23(6): 1073–1102.

Kay, C. (2009) 'Development strategies and rural development: Exploring synergies, eradicating poverty', *Journal of Peasant Studies* 36(1): 103–137.

Keck, M.E. and Sikkink, K. (1998) *Activists Beyond Borders: Advocacy Networks in International Politics*, Cornell University Press, Ithaca (NY).

Kepe, T. and Hall, R. (2018) 'Land redistribution in South Africa: Towards decolonisation or recolonisation?', *Politikon* 45(1): 128–137.

Kerkvliet, B. (2009) 'Everyday politics in peasant societies (and ours)', *Journal of Peasant Studies*, 36(1): 227–243.

Kothari, A., Salleh, A., Escobar, A., Demaria, F. and Acosta, A. (2019) *Pluriverse. A Post-Development Dictionary*, Tulika Books, New Dehli.

Kröger, M. (2021) *Iron Will: Global Extractivism and Mining Resistance in Brazil and India*, University of Michigan Press, Ann Arbor (MI).

Kumar, S. (2021) 'Class, caste and agrarian change: the making of farmers' protests', *Journal of Peasant Studies* 48(7): 1371–1379.

Lahiff, E., Borras Jr, S.M. and Kay, C. (2007) 'Market-led agrarian reform: Policies, performance and prospects', *Third World Quarterly* 28(8): 1417–1436.

Lamb, V. and Dao, N. (2017) 'Perceptions and practices of investment: China's hydropower investments in Vietnam and Myanmar', *Canadian Journal of Development Studies*, 38(3): 395–413.

Lehmann, D. (ed.) (1974) *Peasants, Landlords and Governments: Agrarian Reform in the Third World*, Holmes and Meier Publishers, New York.

Lemisch, J. (2004) 'Cheers for bridging the gap between activism and the academy: Or, stay and fight', in J. Downs and J. Manion (eds), *Taking Back the Academy: History of Activism, History as Activism*, pp. 187–208, Routledge, London.

Lenin, V.I. (2004 [orig. 1905]) *Development of Capitalism in Russia*, University Press of the Pacific, Honolulu (HI).

Lerche, J. (2021) 'The farm laws struggle 2020–2021: class-caste alliances and bypassed agrarian transition in neoliberal India', *Journal of Peasant Studies* 48(7): 1380–1396.

Levien, M. (2013) 'Regimes of dispossession: From steel towns to special economic zones', *Development and Change* 44(2): 381–407.

Levien, M. (2018) *Dispossession Without Development: Land Grabs in Neoliberal India*, Oxford University Press, New York.

Levien, M. (2021) 'Coercive rentier networks: "Land Mafias" in neoliberal India', *Sociology of Development* 7(2): 159–185.

Levien, M., Watts, M. and Yan, H. (2018) 'Agrarian Marxism', *Journal of Peasant Studies* 45(5–6): 853–883.

Levkoe, C. (2021) 'Scholars as allies in the struggle for food systems transformation', *Agriculture and Human Values* 38: 611–614.

Levkoe, C., Brem-Wilson, J. and Anderson, C.R. (2019) 'People, power, change: Three pillars of a food sovereignty research praxis', *Journal of Peasant Studies* 46(7): 1389–1412.

Li, T. (2011) 'Centering labor in the land grab debate', *Journal of Peasant Studies* 38(2): 281–298.

Li, T. (2014) *Land's End: Capitalist Relations on an Indigenous Frontier*, Duke University Press, Durham (NC).

Li, T. (2015) 'Can there be food sovereignty here?', *Journal of Peasant Studies* 42(1) 205–211.

Li, T.M. and Semedi, P. (2021) *Plantation Life: Corporate Occupation in Indonesia's Oil Palm Zone*, Duke University Press, Durham (NC).

Lipton, M. (1977) *Why Poor People Stay Poor: A Study of Urban Bias in World Development*, Temple Smith, London; Australian National University Press, Canberra.

Lund, C. (2016) 'Rule and rupture: State formation through the production of property and citizenship', *Development and Change* 47(6): 1199–1228.

Lund, C. (2021) *Nine-Tenths of the Law*, Yale University Press, New Haven (CT).

Magnan, A., Davidson, M. and Desmarais, A.A. (2022) 'They call it progress, but we don't see it as progress': farm consolidation and land concentration in Saskatchewan, Canada, *Agriculture and Human Values*, 1–14 <https://doi.org/10.1007/s10460-022-10353-y>.

Malseed, K. (2008) 'Where there is no movement: Local resistance and the potential for solidarity', *Journal of Agrarian Change* 8(2–3): 489–514.

Mamonova, N. (2015) 'Resistance or adaptation? Ukrainian peasants' responses to large-scale land acquisitions', *Journal of Peasant Studies* 42(3–4): 607–634.

Mamonova, N. and Sutherland, L.A. (2015) 'Rural gentrification in Russia: Renegotiating identity, alternative food production and social tensions in the countryside', *Journal of Rural Studies* 42: 154–165.

Mao, Z. (1975) 'Preface and postscript to rural surveys', March and April 1941, in *Select Works of Mao Tse-Tung* Vol. III, Foreign Languages Press, Beijing.

Margulis, M.E., McKeon, N. and Borras Jr, S.M. (2013) 'Land grabbing and global governance: Critical perspectives', *Globalizations* 10(1): 1–23.

Martinez-Alier, J., Temper, L., Del Bene, D. and Scheidel, A. (2016) 'Is there a global environmental justice movement?', *Journal of Peasant Studies* 43(3): 731–755.
Martíinez-Alier, J., Healy, H., Temper, L., Walter, M., Rodriguez-Labajos, B., Gerber, J. F. and Conde, M. (2011) 'Between science and activism: learning and teaching ecological economics with environmental justice organisations', *Local Environment* 16(1): 17–36.
Martinez-Torres, M.E. and Rosset, P.M. (2010) 'La Vía Campesina: The birth and evolution of a transnational social movement', *Journal of Peasant Studies* 37(1): 149–175.
Marx, K. (1968 [orig. 1852]) 'The Eighteenth Brumaire of Louis Bonaparte', in *Marx & Engels: Selected Works in One Volume*, pp. 96–166, Lawrence and Wishart, London.
Marx, K. (1983 [orig. 1881]) 'The reply to Zasulich', in T. Shanin (ed.), *Late Marx and the Russian Road*, pp. 123–124, Routledge and Kegan Paul, London.
McCarthy, J. (2019) 'Authoritarianism, populism, and the environment: Comparative experiences, insights, and perspectives', *Annals of the American Association of Geographers* 109(2): 301–313.
McClintock, N. (2014) 'Radical, reformist, and garden-variety neoliberal: Coming to terms with urban agriculture's contradictions', *Local Environment* 19(2): 147–171.
McElwee, P. (2022) 'Advocating afforestation, betting on BECCS: land-based negative emissions technologies (NETs) and agrarian livelihoods in the global South', *Journal of Peasant Studies*, 1–30 <https://doi.org/10.1080/03066150.2022.2117032>.
McKay, B.M. (2017) 'Agrarian extractivism in Bolivia', *World Development* 97: 199–211.
McKay, B.M., Alonso-Fradejas, A. and Ezquerro-Cañete, A. (eds) (2021) *Agrarian Extractivism in Latin America*, Routledge, London.
McKeon, N. (2009) *The United Nations and Civil Society Legitimating Global Governance: Whose Voice?*, Zed, London.
McMichael, P. (2008) 'Peasants make their own history, but not just as they please ...', *Journal of Agrarian Change* 8(2–3): 205–228.
McMichael, P. (2013) *Food Regimes and Agrarian Questions*, Fernwood, Halifax (NS); Practical Action Publishing, Rugby.

McMichael, P. (2020) 'Does China's "going out" strategy prefigure a new food regime?', *Journal of Peasant Studies* 47(1): 116–154.

Mehta, L., Veldwisch, G.J. and Franco, J.C. (2012) 'Introduction to the Special Issue: Water grabbing? Focus on the (re)appropriation of finite water resources', *Water Alternatives* 5(2): 193–207.

Mendez, J.B. (2006) 'Globalizing scholar activism: Opportunities and dilemmas through a feminist lens', in C. Hale (ed.), *Engaging contradictions: Theory, politics, and methods of activist scholarship*, pp. 136–163, University of California Press, Berkeley.

Meyer, D. (2005) 'Scholarship that might matter', in D. Croteau et al. (eds), *Rhyming Hope and History: Activists, Academics, and Social Movement Scholarship*, pp. 191–205, University of Minnesota Press, Minneapolis (MN).

Mills, E.N. (2021) 'The politics of transnational fishers' movements', *Journal of Peasant Studies*, <https://doi.org/10.1080/03066150.2021.1975271>.

Mintz, S. (1973) 'A note on the definition of peasantries', *Journal of Peasant Studies* 1(1): 91–106.

Mitchell, D. (2004) 'Radical scholarship: A polemic on making a difference outside the academy', in D. Fuller and R. Kitchin (eds), *Radical Theory/Critical Praxis: Making a Difference Beyond the Academy*, pp. 21–31, Praxis (e)Press.

Monjane, B. and Bruna, N. (2020) 'Confronting agrarian authoritarianism: Dynamics of resistance to PROSAVANA in Mozambique', *Journal of Peasant Studies* 47(1): 69–94.

Monsalve, S. (2013) 'The human rights framework in contemporary agrarian struggles', *Journal of Peasant Studies* 40(1): 239–290.

Montefrio, M.J.F. and Dressler, W.H. (2016) 'The green economy and constructions of the "idle" and "unproductive" uplands in the Philippines', *World Development* 79: 114–126.

Moore Jr, B. (1967) *Social Origins of Dictatorship and Democracy: Lord and Peasant in the Modern World*, Penguin, Harmondsworth.

Moore, J.W. (2017) 'The Capitalocene, part I: On the nature and origins of our ecological crisis', *Journal of Peasant Studies* 44(3): 594–630.

Moreda, T. (2017) 'Large-scale land acquisitions, state authority and indigenous local communities: Insights from Ethiopia', *Third World Quarterly* 38(3): 698–716.

Moyo, S. (2011) 'Three decades of agrarian reform in Zimbabwe', *Journal of Peasant Studies* 38(3): 493–531.

Moyo, S. and Yeros, P. (eds) (2005) *Reclaiming the Land: The Resurgence of Rural Movements in Africa, Asia and Latin America*, Zed, London.

Moyo, S., Yeros, P. and Jha, P. (2012) 'Imperialism and primitive accumulation: Notes on the new scramble for Africa', *Agrarian South: Journal of Political Economy* 1(2): 181–203.

Moyo, S., Jha, P. and Yeros, P. (2013) 'The classical agrarian question: Myth, reality and relevance today', *Agrarian South: Journal of Political Economy* 2(1): 93–119.

Mudimu, G., Zuo, T. and Nalwimba, N. (2022) 'Inside an enclave: The dynamics of capitalism and rural politics in a post-land reform context', *Journal of Peasant Studies* 49(1): 101–128.

Newell, P. (2022) 'Climate justice', *Journal of Peasant Studies*, 49(5), 915–923.

Newell, P. and Taylor, O. (2018) 'Contested landscapes: The global political economy of climate-smart agriculture', *Journal of Peasant Studies* 45(1): 108–129.

Nikulin, A.M. and Trotsuk, I.V. (2016) 'Utopian visions of contemporary rural–urban Russia', *Third World Thematics: A TWQ Journal* 1(5): 673–690.

Nino, H.P. (2017) 'Migrant workers into contract farmers: Processes of labour mobilization in colonial and contemporary Mozambique', *Africa* 87(1): 79–99.

Nygren, A., Kröger, M. and Gills B. (2022) 'Global extractivisms and transformative alternatives', *Journal of Peasant Studies*, 49:4, 734–759, <https://doi.org/10.1080/03066150.2022.2069495>.

O'Brien, K. and Li, L. (2006) *Rightful Resistance in China*, Cambridge University Press, Cambridge.

Ojeda, D. (2012) 'Green pretexts: Ecotourism, neoliberal conservation and land grabbing in Tayrona National Natural Park, Colombia', *Journal of Peasant Studies* 39(2): 357–375.

O'Laughlin, B. (2008) 'Governing capital? Corporate social responsibility and the limits of regulation', *Development and Change* 39(6): 945–957.

O'Laughlin, B. (2021) 'No separate spheres: the contingent reproduction of living labor in Southern Africa', *Review of International Political Economy*, 1–20 <https://doi.org/10.1080/09692290.2021.1950025>.

Oya, C. (2012) 'Contract farming in sub-Saharan Africa: A survey of approaches, debates and issues', *Journal of Agrarian Change* 12(1): 1–33.

Oya, C. (2013) 'The land rush and classic agrarian questions of capital and labour: A systematic scoping review of the socioeconomic impact of land grabs in Africa', *Third World Quarterly* 34(9): 1532–1557.

Pahnke, A., Tarlau, R. and Wolford, W. (2015) 'Understanding rural resistance: Contemporary mobilization in the Brazilian countryside', *Journal of Peasant Studies* 42(6): 1069–1085.

Paige, J. (1978) *Agrarian Revolution*, Free Press, New York.

Paprocki, K. (2019) 'All that is solid melts into the bay: Anticipatory ruination and climate change adaptation', *Antipode* 51(1): 295–315.

Park, C.M.Y. and White, B. (2017) 'Gender and generation in Southeast Asian agro-commodity booms', *Journal of Peasant Studies* 44(6): 1103–1110.

Patel, R. (2007) *Stuffed and Starved: From Farm to Fork: The Hidden Battle for the World Food System*, Portobello Books.

Patel, R. (2009) 'Grassroots voices: Food sovereignty', *Journal of Peasant Studies* 36(3): 662–706.

Patel, R. and Goodman, J. (2020) 'The long new deal', *Journal of Peasant Studies* 47(3): 431–463.

Pattenden, J. (2018) 'The politics of classes of labour: Fragmentation, reproduction zones and collective action in Karnataka, India', *Journal of Peasant Studies* 45(5–6): 1039–1059.

Pattenden, J. (2023) 'Progressive politics and populism: Classes of labour and rural-urban political sociology: An introduction to the Special Issue', *Journal of Agrarian Change* 23(1): 3–21.

Pelek, D. (2022) 'Ethnic residential segregation among seasonal migrant workers: From temporary tents to new rural ghettos in southern Turkey', *Journal of Peasant Studies* 49(1): 54–77.

Pellegrini, L., Arsel, M., Falconí, F. and Muradian, R. (2014) 'The demise of a new conservation and development policy? Exploring the tensions of the Yasuní ITT initiative', *The Extractive Industries and Society* 1(2): 284–291.

Peluso, N.L. and Lund, C. (2011) 'New frontiers of land control: Introduction', *Journal of Peasant Studies* 38(4): 667–681.

Peluso, N.L., Afiff, S. and Rachman, N.F. (2008) 'Claiming the grounds for reform: Agrarian and environmental movements in Indonesia', *Journal of Agrarian Change* 8(2–3): 377–407.

Perfecto, I. and Vandermeer, J. (2010) 'The agroecological matrix as alternative to the land-sparing/agriculture intensification model', *Proceedings of the National Academy of Sciences* 107(13): 5786–5791.

Peters, C. (2005) 'Knowing what's wrong is not enough: Creating strategy and vision', in D. Croteau et al. (eds), *Rhyming Hope and History: Activists, Academics, and Social Movement Scholarship*, pp. 41–56, University of Minnesota Press, Minneapolis (MN).

Peters, P.E. (2022) 'Struggles over land under customary tenure in contemporary sub-saharan Africa', in S.M. Borras Jr and J.C. Franco (eds), *The Oxford Handbook of Land Politics*, Oxford University Press, Oxford <https://doi.org/10.1093/oxfordhb/9780197618646.013.2>.

Petras, J. and Veltmeyer, H. (2001) 'Are Latin American peasant movements still a force for change?', *Journal of Peasant Studies* 28(2): 83–118.

Pimbert, M. (2009) 'Towards food sovereignty', Gatekeeper series 141, International Institute for Environment and Development, London.

Piven, F.F. (2010) 'Reflections on scholarship and activism', *Antipode* 42(4): 806–810.

Popkin, S. (1979) *The Rational Peasant: The Political Economy of Rural Society in Vietnam*, University of California Press, Berkeley (CA).

Putzel, J. (1995) 'Managing the "main force": The communist party and the peasantry in the Philippines', *Journal of Peasant Studies* 22(4): 645–671.

Pye, O. (2021) 'Agrarian Marxism and the proletariat: A palm oil manifesto', *Journal of Peasant Studies* 48(4): 807–826.

Ra, D. and Ju, K.K. (2021) 'Nothing about us, without us': reflections on the challenges of building Land in Our Hands, a national land network in Myanmar/Burma. *Journal of Peasant Studies* 48(3): 497–516.

Rappaport, J. (2020) *Cowards don't make history: Orlando Fals Borda and the origins of participatory action research*, Duke University Press, Durham, NC.
Ribot, J. (2014) 'Cause and response: Vulnerability and climate in the Anthropocene', *Journal of Peasant Studies* 41(5): 667–705.
Ribot, J. (2022) 'Violent silence: framing out social causes of climate-related crises', *Journal of Peasant Studies*, 49(4), 683–712.
Ribot, J. and Peluso, N. (2003) 'A theory of access', *Rural Sociology* 68(2): 153–181.
Rigg, J., Phongsiri, M., Promphakping, B., Salamanca, A. and Sripun, M. (2020) 'Who will tend the farm? Interrogating the ageing Asian farmer', *Journal of Peasant Studies* 47(2): 306–325.
Robbins, M.J. (2015) 'Exploring the "localization" dimension of food sovereignty', *Third World Quarterly* 36(3): 449–468.
Rodney, W. (2019) *The groundings with my brothers*, Verso Books, New York.
Roman-Alcalá, A. (2015) 'Broadening the land question in food sovereignty to northern settings: A case study of occupy the farm', *Globalizations* 12(4): 545–558.
Roman-Alcalá, A. (2021) 'Agrarian anarchism and authoritarian populism: Towards a more (state-) critical "critical agrarian studies"', *Journal of Peasant Studies* 48(2): 298–328.
Rosset, P. (2013) 'Grassroots voices: Re-thinking agrarian reform, land and territory in La Via Campesina', *Journal of Peasant Studies* 40(4): 721–775.
Rosset, P.M. and Altieri, M.A. (2017) *Agroecology: Science and Politics*, Practical Action Publishing, Rugby.
Routledge, P. and Derickson, K.D. (2015) 'Situated solidarities and the practice of scholar-activism', *Environment and Planning D: Society and Space* 33(3): 391–407.
Sankey, K. (2022) 'We, campesinos: The potentials and pitfalls of agrarian populism in Colombia's agrarian strike', *Journal of Agrarian Change* <https://doi.org/10.1111/joac.12516>.
Sauer, S. and Pereira Leite, S. (2012) 'Agrarian structure, foreign investment in land, and land prices in Brazil', *Journal of Peasant Studies* 39(3–4): 873–898.
Scheidel, A. and Work, C. (2018) 'Forest plantations and climate change discourses: New powers of 'green' grabbing in Cambodia', *Land Use Policy* 77: 9–18.

Scheidel, A., Del Bene, D., Liu, J., Navas, G., Mingorría, S., Demaria, F., ... and Martíinez-Alier, J. (2020) 'Environmental conflicts and defenders: A global overview', *Global Environmental Change* 63: 102104.

Schneider, S. and Niederle, P.A. (2012) 'Resistance strategies and diversification of rural livelihoods: The construction of autonomy among Brazilian family farmers', *Journal of Peasant Studies* 37(2): 379–405.

Scoones, I. (2009a) 'Livelihoods perspectives and rural development', *Journal of Peasant Studies* 36(1): 171–196.

Scoones, I. (2009b) 'The politics of global assessments: the case of the International Assessment of Agricultural Knowledge, Science and Technology for Development (IAASTD)', *Journal of Peasant Studies* 36(3): 547–571.

Scoones, I. (ed) (2010) *Zimbabwe's Land Reform: Myths and Realities*, James Currey, London.

Scoones, I. (2015) *Sustainable Livelihoods and Rural Development*, Fernwood, Halifax (NS); Practical Action Publishing, Rugby.

Scoones, I. (2016) 'The politics of sustainability and development', *Annual Review of Environment and Resources* 41(1): 293–319.

Scoones, I., Amanor, K., Favareto, A. and Qi, G. (eds) (2016) 'A new politics of development cooperation? Chinese and Brazilian engagements in African agriculture', *World Development* 81, special issue.

Scoones, I., Edelman, M., Borras Jr, S. M., Hall, R., Wolford, W. and White, B. (2018) 'Emancipatory rural politics: confronting authoritarian populism', *Journal of Peasant Studies* 45(1): 1–20.

Scoones, I., Smalley, R., Hall, R. and Tsikata, D. (2019) 'Narratives of scarcity: Framing the global land rush', *Geoforum* 101: 231–241.

Scott, J. (1976) *The Moral Economy of the Peasant: Subsistence and Rebellion in Southeast Asia*, Yale University Press, New Haven (CT).

Scott, J. (1985) *Weapons of the weak. Everyday Forms of Peasant Resistance*, Yale University Press, New Haven (CT).

Sekine, Y. (2021) 'Emerging "agrarian climate justice" struggles in Myanmar', *Journal of Peasant Studies* 48(3): 517–540.

Selwyn, B. (2021) 'A green new deal for agriculture: For, within, or against capitalism?', *Journal of Peasant Studies* 48(4): 778–806.

Shah, A. (2022) 'Rethinking "just transitions" from coal: the dynamics of land and labour in anti-coal struggles', *Journal of Peasant Studies*, 1–20 <https://doi.org/10.1080/03066150.2022.2142568>.

Shah, A. and Harriss-White, B. (2011) 'Resurrecting scholarship on agrarian transformations', *Economic and Political Weekly* 46(39): 13–18.

Shah, A. and Lerche, J. (2020) 'Migration and the invisible economies of care: Production, social reproduction and seasonal migrant labour in India', *Transactions of the Institute of British Geographers* 45(4): 719–734.

Shanin, T. (1971) *Peasants and Peasant Societies*, Penguin, London.

Shanin, T. (1972) *The Awkward Class. Political Sociology of Peasantry in a Developing Society Russia 1910–1925*, Clarendon Press, Oxford.

Shanin, T. (1973) 'The nature and logic of the peasant economy 1: A generalisation 1', *Journal of Peasant Studies* 1(1): 63–80.

Shanin, T. (1983a) 'Late Marx: Gods and craftsmen', in T. Shanin (ed), *Late Marx and the Russian Road*, pp. 3–39, Routledge and Kegan Paul, London.

Shanin, T. (1983b) 'Marxism and the vernacular revolutionary traditions', in T. Shanin (ed), *Late Marx and the Russian Road*, pp. 243–279, Routledge and Kegan Paul, London.

Shivji, I.G. (2017) 'The concept of "working people"', *Agrarian South: Journal of Political Economy* 6(1): 1–13.

Siebert, A. (2020) 'Transforming urban food systems in South Africa: Unfolding food sovereignty in the city', *Journal of Peasant Studies* 47(2): 401–419.

Soper, R. (2020) 'From protecting peasant livelihoods to essentializing peasant agriculture: problematic trends in food sovereignty discourse', *Journal of Peasant Studies* 47(2): 265–285.

Sosa Varrotti, A.P. and Gras, C. (2021) 'Network companies, land grabbing, and financialization in South America', *Globalizations* 18(3): 482–497.

Spoor, M. (ed) (2008) *The Political Economy of Rural Livelihoods in Transition Economies: Land, Peasants and Rural Poverty in Transition*, Routledge, London.

Stock, R. and Birkenholtz, T. (2021) 'The sun and the scythe: Energy dispossessions and the agrarian question of labor in solar parks', *Journal of Peasant Studies* 48(5): 984–1007.

Sud, N. (2014) 'The men in the middle: A missing dimension in global land deals', *Journal of Peasant Studies* 41(4): 593–612.

Sudbury, J. and Okazawa-Rey, M. (2009) 'Introduction: Activist scholarship and the neoliberal university', in J. Sudbury and M. Okazawa-Rey (eds), *Activist Scholarship: Antiracism, Feminism, and Social Change*, pp. 1–16, Routledge, New York.

Tadem, E.C. (2016) L*iving in Times of Unrest: Bart Pasion and the Philippine Revolution*, University of the Philippines Press.

Taggart, P. (2000) *Populism*, Open University Press, Milton Keynes.

Tarrow, S. (2005) *The New Transnational Activism*, Cambridge University Press, Cambridge.

Taylor, M. (2018) 'Climate-smart agriculture: What is it good for?', *Journal of Peasant Studies* 45(1): 89–107.

Temudo, M.P. (2012) '"The white men bought the forests": Conservation and contestation in Guinea-Bissau, Western Africa', *Conservation and Society* 10(4): 354–366.

Thompson, E.P. (1971) 'The moral economy of the English crowd in the eighteenth century', *Past & Present* 50: 76–136.

Thompson, E.P. (1991 [orig. 1963]) *The Making of the English Working Class*, Penguin, London.

Thuon, R. (2018) 'Holding corporations from middle countries accountable for human rights violations: A case study of the Vietnamese company investment in Cambodia', *Globalizations* 15(1): 152–167.

Tilzey, M. (2019) 'Authoritarian populism and neo-extractivism in Bolivia and Ecuador: The unresolved agrarian question and the prospects for food sovereignty as counter-hegemony', *Journal of Peasant Studies* 46(3): 626–652.

Torres Contreras, G.A. (2021) 'Twenty-five years under the wind turbines in La Venta, Mexico: Social difference, land control and agrarian change', *Journal of Peasant Studies*, <https://doi.org/10.1080/03066150.2021.1873293>.

Tramel, S. (2016) 'The road through Paris: Climate change, carbon, and the political dynamics of convergence', *Globalizations* 13(6): 960–969.

Tsikata, D. and Yaro, J.A. (2014) 'When a good business model is not enough: Land transactions and gendered livelihood prospects in rural Ghana', *Feminist Economics* 20(1): 202–226.

van der Ploeg, J.D. (2008) *The New Peasantries: Struggles for Autonomy and Sustainability in an Era of Empire and Globalization*, Earthscan, London.

van der Ploeg, J.D. (2013) *Peasants and the Art of Farming: A Chayanovian Manifesto*, Fernwood, Halifax (NS); Practical Action Publishing, Rugby.

van der Ploeg, J.D., Franco, J.C. and Borras Jr, S.M. (2015) 'Land concentration and land grabbing in Europe: A preliminary analysis', *Canadian Journal of Development Studies* 36(2): 147–162.

Veltmeyer, H. (1997) 'New social movements in Latin America: The dynamics of class and identity', *Journal of Peasant Studies* 25(1): 139–69.

Veltmeyer, H. and Petras, J. (2014) *The New Extractivism: A Post-neoliberal Development Model or Imperialism of the Twenty-first Century?* Zed, London.

Vergara-Camus, L. (2014) *Land and Freedom: The MST, the Zapatistas, and Peasant Alternatives to Neoliberalism*, Zed, London.

Verweijen, J. and Marijnen, E. (2018) 'The counterinsurgency/conservation nexus: Guerrilla livelihoods and the dynamics of conflict and violence in the Virunga National Park, Democratic Republic of the Congo', *Journal of Peasant Studies* 45(2): 300–320.

Vigil, S. (2022) *Land Grabs, Environment and Migration in a Changing Climate*, Routledge, London.

Visser, O., Mamonova, N. and Spoor, M. (2012) 'Oligarchs, megafarms and land reserves: Understanding land grabbing in Russia', *Journal of Peasant Studies* 39(3–4): 899–931.

Visser, O., Clapp, J. and Isakson, S.R. (2015) 'Introduction to a symposium on global finance and the agri-food sector: Risk and regulation', *Journal of Agrarian Change* 15(4): 541–548.

Wang, C. and Xu, Y. (2022) 'Reflecting on the Plantationocene: the political economy of sugarcane plantations in Guangxi, China', *Journal of Peasant Studies*, 1–22 <https://doi.org/10.1080/03066150.2022.2087180>.

Weis, T. (2007) *The Global Food Economy: The Battle for the Future of Farming*, Zed, London.

Weis, T. (2010) 'The accelerating biophysical contradictions of industrial capitalist agriculture', *Journal of Agrarian Change* 10(3): 315–341.

Welch, C. and Sauer, S. (2015) 'Rural unions and the struggle for land in Brazil', *Journal of Peasant Studies* 42(6): 1109–1135

White, B. (2016) 'Remembering the Indonesian Peasants' Front and Plantation Workers' Union (1945–1966)', *Journal of Peasant Studies* 43(1): 1–16.

White, B. (2020) *Agriculture and the Generation Problem*, Fernwood, Halifax (NS); Practical Action Publishing, Rugby.

White, B., Borras Jr, S.M., Hall, R., Scoones, I. and Wolford, W. (2012) 'The new enclosures: Critical perspectives on corporate land deals', *Journal of Peasant Studies* 39(3–4): 619–647.

White, M. (2018) *Freedom Farmers: Agricultural Resistance and the Black Freedom Movement*, University of North Carolina Press, Chapel Hill (NC).

Wittman, H., Desmarais, A. and Wiebe, N. (eds) (2010) *Food Sovereignty: Reconnecting Food, Nature & Community*, Fernwood, Halifax (NS); Pambazuka, Oxford.

Wolf, E. (1966) *Peasants*, Prentice-Hall, Englewood Cliffs, US.

Wolf, E. (1969) *Peasant Wars of the Twentieth Century*, University of Oklahoma Press, Norman (OK).

Wolford, W. (2005) 'Agrarian moral economies and neoliberalism in Brazil: Competing worldviews and the state in the struggle for land', *Environment and Planning A: Economy and Space* 37(2): 241–261.

Wolford, W. (2010) *This Land is Ours Now: Social Mobilization and the Meanings of Land in Brazil*, Duke University Press, Durham (NC).

Wolford, W. (2021) 'The Plantationocene: A lusotropical contribution to the theory', *Annals of the American Association of Geographers* 111(6): 1622–1639.

Wolford, W., Borras Jr, S.M., Hall, R., Scoones, I. and White, B. (2013) 'Governing global land deals: The role of the state in the rush for land', *Development and Change* 44(2): 189–210.

Woodhouse, P. (2012) 'New investment, old challenges. Land deals and the water constraint in African agriculture', *Journal of Peasant Studies* 39(3–4): 777–794.

Wright, E.O. (2019) *How to be an Anticapitalist in the Twenty-first Century*, Verso Books, New York.

Wuyts, M. (1994) 'Accumulation, industrialisation and the peasantry: A reinterpretation of the Tanzanian experience', *Journal of Peasant Studies* 21(2): 159–193.

Xiuhtecutli, N. and Shattuck, A. (2021) 'Crisis politics and US farm labor: Health justice and Florida farmworkers amid a pandemic', *Journal of Peasant Studies*, 48(1): 73–98.

Xu, Y. (2019) 'Politics of inclusion and exclusion in the Chinese industrial tree plantation sector: The global resource rush seen from inside China', *Journal of Peasant Studies* 46(4): 767–791.

Yan, H. and Chen, Y. (2015) 'Agrarian capitalization without capitalism? Capitalist dynamics from above and below in China', *Journal of Agrarian Change* 15(3): 366–391.

Yan, H., Bun, K.H. and Siyuan, X. (2021) 'Rural revitalization, scholars, and the dynamics of the collective future in China', *Journal of Peasant Studies* 48(4): 853–874.

Yaşın, Z. (2022) 'The environmentalization of the agrarian question and the agrarianization of the climate justice movement', *Journal of Peasant Studies* 49(7): 1355–1386.

Ye, J. (2015) 'Land transfer and the pursuit of agricultural modernization in China', *Journal of Agrarian Change* 15(3): 314–337.

Ye, J., van der Ploeg, J.D., Schneider, S. and Shanin, T. (2020) 'The incursions of extractivism: Moving from dispersed places to global capitalism', *Journal of Peasant Studies* 47(1): 155–183.

Yeh, E., O'Brien, K. and Ye, J. (2013) 'Rural politics in contemporary China', *Journal of Peasant Studies* 40(6), special issue.

Zasulich, V. (1983 [orig. 1881]) 'A letter to Marx', in T. Shanin (ed), *Late Marx and the Russian Road*, pp. 98–99, Routledge and Kegan Paul, London.

Zoomers, A. (2010) 'Globalisation and the foreignisation of space: Seven processes driving the current global land grab', *Journal of Peasant Studies* 37(2): 429–447.

Zoomers, A. and van der Haar G. (eds) (2000) *Current Land Policy in Latin America: Regulating Land Tenure Under Neo-Liberalism*, Royal Tropical Institute (KIT), Amsterdam.

www.ingramcontent.com/pod-product-compliance
Ingram Content Group UK Ltd.
Pitfield, Milton Keynes, MK11 3LW, UK
UKHW060455150426
5217IPUK00028B/2081